MW00945097

GOD IS GREATER THAN YOU THINK

A former Mormon explains why he left the
Mormon Church and why he can never return

Wade Wadsworth

Edited by Paul Engberson

WESTBOW
PRESS®
A DIVISION OF THOMAS NELSON
& ZONDERVAN

WestBow Press books may be ordered through booksellers or by contacting:

WestBow Press
A Division of Thomas Nelson & Zondervan
1663 Liberty Drive
Bloomington, IN 47403
www.westbowpress.com
1 (866) 928-1240

Scripture taken from the King James Version of the Bible.

ISBN: 978-1-9736-7026-1 (sc)
ISBN: 978-1-9736-7025-4 (hc)
ISBN: 978-1-9736-7027-8 (e)

Library of Congress Control Number: 2019910740

Print information available on the last page.

WestBow Press rev. date: 8/20/2019

ACKNOWLEDGMENTS

As friends, Paul Engberson and I shared the experiences of boyhood—bicycles, BB guns, exploring the desert, fishing, camping overnight at each other's homes, and many other experiences of growing up together as neighbors in rural Idaho. It is with warm memories and deep appreciation that I say thank you to Paul for his indispensable editing suggestions.

Appreciation is also in order for the folks at WestBow Press for their expertise, patience, perseverance, and kindness as I, a fledgling author, worked through the necessary changes to make this book publishable.

And special appreciation to my lovely wife, April, who patiently shared her husband with hundreds of hours of reading, study, writing, and reviewing.

CONTENTS

PREFACE

In John 17:3, the Lord Jesus Christ defined eternal life: "And this is life eternal that they might know Thee, the only true God, and Jesus Christ, whom thou hast sent."

I was born into the Church of Jesus Christ of Latter-Day Saints. I was active in the church as a youth, but as I grew older, there seemed to be some things about Mormon teaching that did not ring true to me. I began to search for answers, thinking that the problem was with me or some views held by members of our local ward and that I just needed more enlightenment.

I wrote to the president of the church, at that time David O. McKay, and asked him the specific things about which I was concerned. The letter was referred to my stake presidency[1] who in turn invited me to discuss my concerns with them.

During our discussion, one member of the stake presidency gave me this advice: "Wade, if you find something better, join it." He was confident that in all my searching, it would not be possible for me to find any church better than the Church of Jesus Christ of Latter-Day Saints. What I did find, however, was better than any organized church ever could be. I found the one true God of whom the Lord Jesus Christ spoke in John 17:3.

Since leaving the Mormon Church, I have experienced concern and curiosity from Mormon people who did not understand my decision. I want to explain my reasons for leaving the Mormon Church and why I can never return. This book is not intended to be an exhaustive study on either Mormon doctrine or Christian theology. It simply explains some of the things I have learned about the only true God and contrasts biblical teachings with the teachings, works, and prophecies of the prophet Joseph Smith.

My leaving the Mormon Church was a decision of great importance with far-reaching consequences. I assure you that I did not do it suddenly or without much soul searching, prayer, and guidance from the scriptures. Some of the things I say here will not be easy to read if you are a member of the Church of Jesus Christ of Latter-Day Saints. In fact, it may try your soul, as it did mine. In the end, you might disagree. But I ask of you this one thing—please, let me explain.

CHAPTER 1

SEARCHING FOR THE TRUE GOD

The God I know and serve is so wonderful. He is so holy and righteous that the apostle John said in 1 John 1:5, "God is light, and in Him is no darkness at all."

Because God is holy, He will not accept sin of any kind. He is a just God, and with Him, justice must prevail. That is why God is also a God of wrath. Many times, God has revealed His righteous wrath against those who refuse to repent. This is true with individuals, cities, and nations.

The Bible tells us that all are sinners. Romans 3:10–12 says,

> As it is written, there is none righteous, no not one: There is none that understandeth, there is none that seeketh after God. They are all gone out of the way, they are together become unprofitable; there is none that doeth good, no not one.

That is hard to accept, but I know it is true of me because God's Word declares it. Verse 23 says, "For all have sinned and come short of the glory of God." I am convinced that the "all" of verse 23 includes me.

As a boy, I learned I could not live even the Boy Scout Law let alone all of God's Law. When I understand that God is holy and that I am a sinner, I am faced with the horrible fact that God's righteous wrath will one day be poured out on me. He is a just God. He can do nothing less. He must punish me for my sin. That is justice.

However, God is also love (1 John 4:8, 16). In that wonderful truth, I find hope. Romans 5:8 tells us, "God commendeth his love toward us in that, while we were yet sinners Christ died for us." God's love for me is so great that it can be measured only in what He gave to me to rescue me from His necessary wrath for my sin. If God forgave me without someone taking the punishment I deserve, He would be circumventing or violating His justice and would no longer be holy and just. For God to forgive, someone had to take my just punishment, the punishment I deserve.

God gave His only Son to die on the cross for us; He paid our sin debt so He could forgive us and remain just and holy. What is so wonderful to me is that He did not have to do it. It would have been so easy for the all-powerful God to have destroyed the world when the horrible ugliness of sin first appeared. He could have simply wiped the planet out of existence and started again with a new race of people. The Genesis flood is a clear example of just how easily He could have done this. But He didn't. Even in a time of judgment, he preserved humankind because He loves us.

He loves you. He looked into the future and saw you, me, and everyone else. God thought in His heart, *I want you to be mine, to live with Me for all eternity. I love you with an everlasting love.* And so, God sent His only begotten Son to die on the cross for each one of us (1 Peter 2:24).

God loves you with all the love He has for everyone else. Jesus Christ has done all the work of redemption on the cross. To receive forgiveness of our sins, He asks only that we believe in Him, what He has done for us, turn from our sin, and ask Him for forgiveness. Ephesians 2:8–9 makes it very clear: "For by grace are ye saved through faith; and that not of yourselves, it is the gift of God—not of works, lest any man should boast." Notice that forgiveness of sin is not earned by works; rather, it is a gift. Of course, the question of faith and works and how good works relate to God's plan probably comes to your mind. We will discuss that in chapter 6.

When we talk about God and the Son of God, Jesus Christ, we must be sure we understand each other. Are we really talking about the same God and the same Son of God? I ask this question because of the vast difference between what the prophet Isaiah and the prophet Joseph Smith taught. In John 17:3, Jesus said, "And this is life eternal, that they might know thee, the only true God, and Jesus Christ, whom thou hast sent." Jesus said that there was only one true God, which is what Isaiah taught. But in contrast, Joseph Smith taught a plurality of gods. Let me explain.

First of all, does the Bible support the position that there is a plurality of gods? There are several places in the Bible where it mentions gods plural. One such passage is 1 Corinthians 8:4–6.

> As concerning, therefore, eating of those things that are offered in sacrifice to idols, we know that an idol is nothing in the world, and that there is no other God but one. For though there be that are called gods, whether in heaven or in earth (as there are gods many, and lords many), but to us there is but one God, the Father, of whom are all things, and we in him; and one Lord Jesus Christ by whom are all things, and we by him.

The subject of these verses is that of eating things sacrificed to idols. We find the word *God* used in two ways. It is capitalized when referring to the one God of heaven, the Father. It is lowercased when referring to the many idols of the world. This method was used throughout the Bible to avoid confusion. In Paul's day, the Greeks worshipped some 30,000 such gods.

We see this also borne out in Psalm 96:4–5, which contrasts the difference between the Lord and the gods of the nations, which were mere idols. "For the LORD is great, and greatly to be praised; he is to be feared above all gods. For all the gods of the nations are idols; but the LORD made the heavens."

On occasion, the word *gods* is used in reference to human judges. It is translated from the Hebrew word *elohim*, literally, "strong ones." It was applied to human judges because of their position. In Psalm 82:1–4, we find an example of this use where Israel's judges were being chastised for not defending the fatherless and needy against the wicked.

> God standeth in the congregation of the mighty;
> he judgeth among the gods. How long will ye judge
> unjustly and accept the persons of the wicked? Selah.
> Defend the poor and the fatherless: do justice to the
> afflicted and needy. Deliver the poor and needy out of
> the hand of the wicked.

This is speaking of human judges. We must understand this when interpreting the Bible so we do not confuse God the Father with pagan gods.

Let's see what the only true God declares about Himself in the Bible. The prophet Isaiah was prophesying during a time of severe spiritual deterioration in Israel. Many were worshipping idols, and God was warning that judgment was coming in the form of captivity in Babylon. Again and again, God tells Israel who He is and that there are no others like Him.

> Ye are my witnesses, saith the LORD, and my servant
> whom I have chosen, that ye may know and believe
> me, and understand that I am he; before me there was
> no God formed, neither shall there be after me. (Isaiah
> 43:10)

> Thus saith the LORD, the King of Israel, and his redeemer
> the Lord of hosts; I am the first, and I am the last; and
> beside me there is no God. Fear not, neither be afraid;
> have not I told thee from that time, and have declared it?
> Ye are even my witnesses. Is there a God beside me? Yea,
> there is no God; I know not any. (Isaiah 44:6, 8)

> I am the LORD, and there is none else, there is no God
> beside me: I girded thee, though thou hast not known
> me. (Isaiah 45:5)

> Look unto me, and be saved, all the ends of the earth:
> for I am God, and there is none else. (Isaiah. 45:22)

Other passages could be quoted, but it can be seen from these that God is clearly stating that He is the only God in existence. He is the only God who ever existed, and He is the only God who will ever exist. We find elsewhere in the Old Testament that God has always existed as God and does not change.

> Before the mountains were brought forth, or ever thou hadst formed the earth and the world, even from everlasting to everlasting, thou art God. (Psalm 90:2)

> For I am the LORD, I change not; therefore ye sons of Jacob are not consumed. (Malachi 3:6)

> Every good gift and every perfect gift is from above, and cometh down from the Father of lights, with whom is no variableness, neither shadow of turning. (James 1:17)

Down through the centuries, Christianity has held the same view of God as did the prophet Isaiah and the other biblical writers. The prophet Joseph Smith taught something entirely different. He taught that God was once a man and progressed to where he is today. He also taught that we have wrongly imagined that God has been God from all eternity. Obviously, God's eternal existence is not something humanity has imagined; it has been declared by God Himself in the Bible.

It is my understanding that Joseph Smith further taught that not only was God once a man, but He was before that a spirit child as well. He was born on a planet and took on a human body; because he lived in obedience to his Father, He was exalted to the position of godhood. The doctrine of eternal progression teaches that people on earth today can one day be exalted to godhood if they obey all the laws and ordinances of the Mormon gospel.[1]

The prophet Isaiah believed in and served the God who has existed from all eternity, never changes, and declares there is and never will be another God. The prophet Joseph Smith believed in and served what he believed to be an exalted man who was eternally progressing, one god among many who would see at least some of his offspring become gods like himself. Only those who have not studied and understood the writings of both prophets could assume that both men believed in the same God. Obviously, they did not. This vast difference in their beliefs separates Isaiah from Joseph Smith so far apart in their spiritual and eternal direction that they cannot possibly arrive at the same place after the judgment of God.

Suppose that Isaiah and Joseph Smith were contemporaries and had a long journey to take. One had a horse and the other only imagined he had a horse. They departed, and the one on the horse rode off. The one who had imagined he had a horse was left behind no matter how strongly he believed he had a horse. It would make a great deal of difference in such an instance whether a man had a horse or only thought he did. When Joseph Smith and Isaiah stand before God to be judged, one will be greatly rewarded for his faith and the great work he has done. The other will discover that the god he only thought was there in fact did not exist. He will be held guilty for worshipping a false god and teaching others to do likewise.

When the apostle Peter was examined by Jewish leaders for healing a lame man, he spoke to them about Jesus Christ and said there was salvation in no other.

> Be it known unto you all, and to all the people of Israel, that by the name of Jesus Christ of Nazareth, whom ye crucified, whom God raised from the dead, even by him doth this man stand here before you whole. This is the stone which was set at naught of you builders, which is become the head of the corner. Neither is there salvation in any other; for there is no other name under heaven given among men, whereby we must be saved. (Acts 4:10–12)

Clearly, there is no hope of salvation outside Jesus Christ. There is salvation in no other. But which Jesus Christ is the real one? Which one is the true Savior? Oh yes, there will be more than one Jesus Christ. The Lord Himself warned us about them: "For there shall arise false Christs and false prophets, and shall shew great signs and wonders, insomuch that, if it were possible, they shall deceive the very elect" (Matthew 24:24). Because Joseph Smith presents a different god than does the Bible, he also presents a different Christ than does the Bible. The diagram below makes this more apparent.

Eternal God	Exalted Man
One and only eternal unchanging God	Ever progressing exalted man, one of many gods
God's eternal Son Jesus Christ	An exalted man's son named Jesus Christ
Salvation in no other	Salvation in no other

On the left is Jesus Christ, the Son of the eternal, unchanging God. On the right is Jesus Christ, the son of an ever-progressing, exalted man, just one god among many. Which Jesus Christ did Peter say was the only hope of salvation? Certainly, Jesus Christ could not be the son of both Fathers. Which Jesus is the real one? You can see it is of utmost importance to find out.

> The God of Isaiah emphatically stated that the gods of Joseph Smith did not exist: "Fear ye not, neither be afraid: have not I told thee from that time, and have declared it? Ye are even my witnesses, is there a God beside me? Yea, there is no God; I know not any" (Isaiah 44:8).

Was it the prophet Isaiah or the prophet Joseph Smith who served the true God of heaven? It is imperative that we find out. But to do so, we must first know for sure whether the Bible and the Book of Mormon are both the Word of God. If we were to rely on words that were not given by the true God of heaven, we would be unable to discover the truth.

CHAPTER 2

DISCOVERING THE WORD OF GOD

Is the Bible really true? That is a fundamental question that must be answered since so many people rely on the Bible as a source of divine truth. You have probably heard many arguments against the Bible: "Don't you know the Bible is full of myth and legend? Don't you know that the Bible has been copied and recopied hundreds of times with each scribe adding his own ideas? Don't you know that the Bible is mistranslated? Don't you know the Bible contradicts itself?" Thus the arguments go.

One of Satan's subtle tactics in his battle against the truth is to attack the Word of God by casting doubt and suspicion on it. In Genesis 3:1–5, Satan brings a subtle accusation against the Word of God: "Yea, hath God said …" The devil is insinuating that God is not truthful. "Did God really say that, Eve? Come on, you don't really believe that, do you?" he suggests.

God had told Adam and Eve not to eat of the forbidden fruit; He said that they would die if they did. In Genesis 3:4, Satan flatly tells Eve that is not true: "Ye shall not surely die." He is cleverly suggesting that Eve will be wiser if she eats the forbidden fruit. The enemy has led men astray through the centuries by such subtle suggestions, hints— anything to cast doubt and suspicion on God's Word. That is the way of a deceiver—accusation without conclusive proof.

Isaiah 43:10 tells us that we are to know and believe God. If the Bible is in fact God's Word, it is through the Bible that we can come to know the only true God and believe in all He tells us of Himself. Let's examine a small portion of the evidence.

> There are now more than 5,300 known Greek manuscripts
> of the New Testament. Add over 10,000 Latin Vulgate
> and at least 9,300 other early versions (MSS) and we have
> more than 24,000 manuscript copies of portions of the
> New Testament in existence today. No other document
> of antiquity even begins to approach such numbers and
> attestation. In comparison, the Iliad by Homer is second
> with only 643 manuscripts that still survive.[1]

Through textual criticism, the scientific study of the manuscripts, we can determine what was written in the original writings. Textual criticism involves a meticulous comparison of manuscript with manuscript and wording with wording to discover any variations. If there were only a few manuscripts with which this scientific examination could be made, there would be a possibility of error. However, we do not have just a few manuscripts; we have literally thousands. In addition to those cited above, we have 36,289 quotations of the New Testament by the church fathers[2] (also called the apostolic fathers—men who led the church right after the apostles died). J. Harold Greenlee said that the quotations of the scripture in the works of the early Christian writers were "so extensive that the N.T. could virtually be reconstructed from them without the use of New Testament manuscripts."[3]

We should not be surprised to learn that God has seen fit to preserve His Word so perfectly for us. Jesus said in Matthew 5:18, "'Till heaven and earth pass, one jot or one tittle shall in no wise pass from the law." In Luke 16:17, He said, "It is easier for heaven and earth to pass, than one tittle of the law to fail." A jot and a tittle are small portions of some Hebrew letters like the dotting of an *i* or the crossing of a *t*. The meaning is obvious—God will not allow His message to humanity to lose one letter of its intended meaning.

Though the Old Testament was originally written in Hebrew and a small portion in Aramaic, it was translated into Greek around 250 BC. This is the Bible Jesus and the people of His day used in addition to the Hebrew text. In Mark 7:9, Jesus said, "Full well ye reject the commandment of

God, that ye may keep your own tradition." Jesus was referring to the Old Testament, and He called it the "commandment of God." Our Lord used the Old Testament for His standard of personal living and for authority in ministry. In Matthew 21:13, when He said, "It is written My house shall be called a house of prayer, but ye have made it a den of thieves," He was quoting Isaiah 56:7.

Three times when He was tempted in the wilderness by Satan, He said, "It is written …" and then quoted Deuteronomy 8:13, 6:16, 6:13, and 10:20. In Luke 24:25–27, Jesus speaks to two disciples on the road from Jerusalem to Emmaus after His resurrection about what the prophets had written about Him. In verse 44, He includes the psalms and the writings.

Because of His love and concern for us, the Lord Jesus Christ warned us of the hypocrites', the Pharisees', and other Jewish leaders' false teaching. He also warned us of false prophets and false christs. But He is found nowhere warning us about the Old Testament. He did not discredit the manuscripts that were relied upon at that time. He did not discredit the Septuagint translation. He never said not to trust the Old Testament as God's Word. If God's Word had been inaccurate at that time, He could easily have said, "Forget the Old Testament. I am a higher authority. Listen only to Me," but He did not. He relied on the Old Testament; He put it on the same level as His own words. He called it scripture (Luke 4:21), truth (John 17:17), God's Word (Mark 7:13), and God's Commandments (Mark 7:9). He based His ministry on it and to identify Himself as the Messiah (Isaiah 61:1–2; compare Luke 4:16–21).

Today, we have Hebrew manuscripts of the Old Testament. We also have the Dead Sea Scrolls, which assure us of the accuracy of the manuscripts we had before that. And we have the Septuagint version of the Old Testament. Also, we have tremendous archeological evidence and virtually hundreds of fulfilled prophecies that also assure us of the accuracy of the Old Testament. If the Lord Jesus had no problem accepting the Old Testament, I certainly do not.

The Lord Jesus Christ also assured us that the New Testament could be relied on. He promised the Holy Ghost to the apostles for inspiration. This promise was made while Jesus and the apostles were in the upper room shortly before the crucifixion. He promised them the Comforter, the Spirit of Truth in John 14:16–17 and 26.

Jesus repeated His promise after His resurrection in Acts 1:5–9. The promise was fulfilled in Acts 2:1–4 when the Holy Ghost came to the apostles, who were waiting as the Lord had instructed them to. We also know that the Lord handpicked His apostles; He made that clear in John 15:16: "Ye have not chosen me, but I have chosen you, and ordained you, that ye should go and bring forth much fruit, and that your fruit should remain."

Other passages in the Gospels describe His actual choosing of the twelve (Matthew 10:1–4; Mark 6:7–13; Luke 9:1–6). The apostles reaffirmed this as Paul claimed inspiration for himself in 1 Corinthians 2:13 and put himself and the other apostles on the same level as the prophets of old in Ephesians 2:20. Peter put Paul's writings on the same level as other scripture in 2 Peter 3:15–16.

Someone might ask, "All right, so the books of the Bible are accurate, but how do we know that the books we have are really the ones God wanted us to have?" The early Christians who selected the books of the Bible did not choose those books they thought they would like as a matter of personal preference. Their task was to discover or recognize the books that were inspired. To do that, they had certain criteria by which the books and letters had to be measured.

- Is it authoritative? Did it come from the hand of God? Does this book come with a divine "Thus saith the Lord"?
- Is it prophetic? Was it written by a man of God?
- Is it authentic? The fathers had the policy of "if in doubt, throw it out." This enhanced the validity of their discernment of canonical books.
- Is it dynamic? Did it come with the life-transforming power of God?
- Was it received, collected, and used? Was it accepted by the people of God? Peter acknowledged Paul's work as scripture parallel to Old Testament scripture (2 Peter 3:16).[4]

A great deal of time and painstaking work was invested in recognizing the sixty-six books of the Bible as the ones that were inspired. Through the centuries, various ones have come under scrutiny again, but none have been found wanting.

Whenever the enemy attacks the Word of God and sneers, "Yeah, hath God said?" I can answer with confidence, "Yes, God has said." It has been proven conclusively many times and in many ways that the Bible is in fact God's written Word. Each time the evil one says, "Don't you know the Bible is full of myth and legend, is mistranslated, has been recopied so many times it is unreliable" and so on, I can rest assured that God has not lied or failed to keep His Word: "Heaven and earth shall pass away, but my words shall not pass away" (Matthew 24:35).

A word needs to be said about translations. There are many English translations today, and the Bible has been translated into over 1,300 other languages. God is not afraid to have the Bible examined in the minutest detail. The Hebrew and Greek texts are available for those who wish to study them in depth, and as long as the texts are available, God's people will continue to study and translate the Bible.

Hundreds of scholars and thousands of pastors and Bible teachers have searched the original Bible languages to discover God's message. This is a very healthy situation; that way, no one person or group can prevent the majority from having access to the Word of God as has happened and does happen in some countries. Also, with so many studying and translating, it is impossible for any person or group to impose false teaching on everyone. We can thank God that He has made His Word so abundantly available to us.

EXAMINING THE BOOK OF MORMON

When I contemplate placing my faith in the Book of Mormon on the same level as the Bible, I ask, "Does it measure up to the Bible? Is it really true? Can it stand the test of close scrutiny?"

The Book of Mormon is a unique book. The Bible makes the claim of being inspired. That inspiration of course was in the original writings, not in the copies or the translations. However, Joseph Smith claimed that the actual "translation" of the Book of Mormon was inspired—that is, it was translated by the gift and power of God in such a way that it was not necessary for any human participant to have any knowledge whatsoever about the language in which the Book of Mormon was written.[5]

I know no other book for which such a claim is made. That claim sets the Book of Mormon apart from all other books. If the Book of Mormon was translated by the gift and power of God as Joseph Smith asserted,[6] then it had to be an absolutely perfect translation. God could do no less.

Wilford C. Wood, a faithful member of the Mormon Church, made available the original 1830 edition of the Book of Mormon in a book entitled *Joseph Smith Begins His Work, Volume I.* You should be able to easily obtain a copy to check the comparisons I make in the following paragraphs. An exhaustive comparison of the 1830 edition with the 1964 edition has revealed over 3,900 changes.[7] Many of those changes are changes in spelling and grammar and do not change the meaning of the text, but other changes are more significant.

In 1 Nephi 8:4, words have been added. The 1830 edition reads "But, behold, Laman and Lemuel, I fear exceedingly, because of you; for behold, me thought I saw a dark and dreary wilderness" (1830 edition, 18). The 1964 edition reads, "But, behold, Laman and Lemuel, I fear exceedingly, because of you; behold, me thought I saw **in my dream** a dark and dreary wilderness"[8] (emphasis added).

Words were also added to 1 Nephi 8:18: "And it came to pass that I saw them, but they would not come unto me" (1830 edition, 19). Compare that with the 1964 edition: "And it came to pass that I saw them, but they would not come unto me **and partake of my fruit**"[9] (emphasis added).

An addition of five words was made to 1 Nephi 19:20. First, the 1964 edition: "For had not the Lord been merciful, to show unto me concerning them, even as he had prophets of old, **I should have perished also**" (emphasis added). Compare that with the 1830 edition (52): "For had not the Lord been merciful, to show unto me concerning them, even as he had prophets of old; for he surely did shew unto the prophets of old …"[10]

In 1 Nephi 20:1, **"Or out of the waters of Baptism"**[11] (emphasis added) has been added (compare 1830 edition, 52, the last three lines).

In Mosiah 28:17, the word *back* was inserted between the words *time* and *until*[12] causing significant change in meaning (1830 edition, 216, last paragraph).

Words were deleted from some passages such as Mosiah 29:15.[13] The 1830 edition reads as follows: "Him have I punished **according to the crime which he hath committed** according to the law which hath been given to us by our fathers" (1830 edition, 218, first paragraph, emphasis added). Examining the 1964 text reveals these words: "Him have I punished according to the law which has been given to us by our fathers."

The degree of change in meaning caused by these word changes is not my first concern. My first concern is whether the words were added to or deleted from the original writing, i.e., the gold plates from which the Book of Mormon was supposedly translated. How do we know if they were or were not? It is claimed that the Book of Mormon was the only book translated "by the gift and power of God."[14] That claim calls for close scrutiny; is it just an empty claim, or can it be substantiated by fact?

When were the changes made and by whom? If they were made by Joseph Smith, did he have the gold plates (assuming they existed) and the *urim* and *thummim*[15] when he made the corrections? If not, by what power, knowledge, or authority did he make the changes? If we were to assume he had been again endowed with some special gift of God to make the changes, we are still left with the dilemma as to why God's gift and power were insufficient to make a correct translation the first time. If the changes made are accurate and true to the original writing on the gold plates, we must concede that the first translation was faulty. If the original translation was in fact by the gift and power of God as claimed, it was a perfect translation and the changes that have been made were therefore unauthorized by God and destroyed the integrity of the text.

Assuming for the moment that the original writings on the gold plates were inspired by God and wholly true, it is still obvious that the Book of Mormon used today is not wholly true. How can we know which portions are true and which are not? Without the gold plates, we have no way to find out. I cannot risk my eternal future on any writing that is proven so inaccurate and untrustworthy.

The Book of Mormon has other problems. The fact that the gold plates are not available is one. With the Bible, God elected to leave us a vast number of manuscripts that every generation of Christians can study and compare to their hearts' content. In the case of the Book of Mormon, we have no manuscripts to examine. We must accept without evidence that either the original 1830 edition was the correct translation or that the later editions with their changes are the correct ones. And we don't know which if either is correct.

And to add to this, the Book of Mormon admits to error in the original writing. Mormon 9:33 says, "And if our plates had been sufficiently large, we should have written in Hebrew; but the Hebrew hath been altered by us also and if we could have written in Hebrew, behold, ye would have had no imperfections in our record."[16] The statement is plain; being forced to write on limited space resulted in "imperfections in our record." Even if we had the gold plates, there would be no way of ever discovering what or where those imperfections are.

For those who have placed their faith in the Book of Mormon, these facts are very unsettling or should be. However, I am convinced that God loves every one of us and that we can be sure He wants us to have His truth. Those born into and raised in the Church of Jesus Christ of Latter-Day Saints have strong feelings about the Book of Mormon. Discovering that there are serious problems in it can cause a tremendous inner struggle; it can cause troubling doubts perhaps resulting in frustration and anger. I have been through years of that kind of struggle in search of God's truth, and I can assure you once again that God loves you more than you can imagine. He will never lie to you. He will never deceive you. It is not God who caused the problems in the Book of Mormon. Simply ask Him to lead you into all truth and He will even though the road ahead may be difficult.

Those who have been born Hindu, Buddhist, or Muslim also have feelings of allegiance to their faiths, but that does not make them right. Religious feelings do not make us right or wrong even though they are powerful. Only God is right, and we must seek Him. Proverbs 14:12 says, "There is a way that seemeth right unto a man, but the end thereof are the ways of death." We must learn to trust in God and not in the feelings of our hearts that can be unpredictable and changing. "Trust in the Lord with all thine heart and lean not unto thine own understanding. In all thy ways acknowledge Him and He shall direct thy paths" (Proverbs 3:5–6). Only by trusting in the Lord are we safe.

Please let me explain further why I cannot believe the Book of Mormon to be the Word of God. In Mormon 9:32–34, it is said that the Book of Mormon was written in a language called reformed Egyptian,[17] that the language was known to "none other people," and that God had "prepared means for the interpretation thereof." In Joseph Smith's account of the translation of the Book of Mormon in the *Pearl of Great Price* Martin Harris took the characters Joseph Smith had copied from the plates to Professor Anthon, "a man celebrated for his literary attainments." Anthon stated that the translation was correct "more so than any he had before seen translated from Egyptian." Martin Harris continued, "I then showed him those that were not translated and he said that they were Egyptian, Chaldaic, Assyriac and Arabic; and he said they were true characters." It is said also that a Dr. Mitchell "sanctioned what Professor Anthon had said respecting both the characters and the translation."[18]

If reformed Egyptian was not known to anyone (which necessitated the use of the seer stone to translate it), how could Anthon and Mitchell read it and say the translation was accurate? The Rosetta Stone, discovered in 1799, was the key that unlocked Egyptian hieroglyphics, but no reformed Egyptian has ever been found anywhere. Hypothetically, it is possible that only the gold plates were reformed Egyptian. But the question still remains—how did Mitchell and Anthon know reformed Egyptian? How could they read it? How could they testify that the translation was accurate if they had never seen the language?

In Alma 7:10, we read that the Son of God was to be born in Jerusalem.[19] The Bible prophesies in Micah 5:2 that Christ would be born in Bethlehem, and the fulfillment is recorded in Matthew 2:1. An explanation has been offered that Alma 7:10 means Christ would be born in the land of Jerusalem, but having studied Palestinian geography and Bible history, I find no land of Jerusalem. The land surrounding Jerusalem and Bethlehem during the time of Christ's birth was the

Roman province of Judea. Jerusalem is a city, not a land or a province. Alma's prophecy failed in its accuracy.

We find a direct contradiction in 2 Nephi 5:15–16.

> And I did teach my people to build buildings, and to work in all manner of wood, and of iron, and copper, and of brass, and of steel, and of gold, and of silver, and of precious ores, *which were in great abundance.* And I, Nephi, did build a temple; and I did construct it after the manner of the temple of Solomon save it were not built of so many precious things; *for they were not to be found upon the land* wherefore, it could not be built like unto Solomon's temple. (emphasis added)[20]

These are only a few examples of the hundreds of serious problems that are known in the Book of Mormon.

Perhaps you are asking, "So what does all this prove? The Book of Mormon was prophesied in the Bible, so it has to be true." Let's look at Ezekiel 37, said to be a prophecy predicting the Book of Mormon. The chapter begins with Ezekiel's vision of the valley of dry bones, an illustration of the nation of Israel scattered and later regathered. The vision is explained in verses 11–14. Israel as a nation rejected Christ and was scattered among the nations of the earth a second time after AD 70, when Jerusalem was destroyed by the Romans. From then until 1948, when the State of Israel was reestablished, they had no land and were in a hopeless condition as far as a nation was concerned. The prophecy in Ezekiel 37 tells of the restoration of Israelites to the land of Israel, and we are witnessing the fulfillment of that return today as the Jews gather in Israel.

After the end of Solomon's reign, Israel was divided into two kingdoms (1 Kings 12). One kingdom was in the north, where ten tribes occupied the northern parts of Israel. Two tribes stayed in the south and occupied the area called Judea in Christ's time. The two sticks in Ezekiel 37:15–20 represent the northern and southern kingdoms; they do not represent the Bible and the Book of Mormon as has been asserted by the Mormon Church. Read the whole chapter and let it speak for itself. Verse 21 makes it clear that nations, not books, are being discussed: "And I make them one nation in the land upon the mountains of Israel, and one king shall be king to them all; and they shall be no more two nations, neither shall they be divided into two kingdoms any more at all." This was first fulfilled with Israel's return from Babylon. If you were to go to Israel today, you would find only one Jewish nation; it is no longer divided. God is fulfilling the prophecy of Ezekiel 37 by bringing the two kingdoms together.

The Mormon eighth article of faith reads as follows: "We believe the Bible to be the word of God as far as it is translated correctly; we also believe the book of Mormon to be the word of God." If anyone has serious doubts about a certain portion of the Bible being mistranslated, the manuscripts and the linguistic skills are available to check that out.

The problems I have outlined concerning the Book of Mormon run much deeper than simple errors in translation, and there is no recourse to solve the problems. There are no manuscripts or gold plates, no one knows reformed Egyptian—if there ever was such a language— and the seer stones are not available if they ever existed. Therefore, I have decided not to accept the Book of Mormon as the Word of the only true God.

CHAPTER 3

THE PROOF OF PROPHECY

The Bible repeatedly declares that the only true God is a righteous God. Here are a few examples.

> Therefore hath the LORD watched upon the evil, and brought it upon us: for the LORD our God *is* righteous in all his works which he doeth: for we obeyed not his voice. (Daniel 9:14)

> And I heard the angel of the waters say, Thou art righteous, O Lord, who art, and wast, and shalt be, because thou hast judged thus. (Revelation 16:5)

As Jesus prayed to the Father in heaven, He addressed Him as "O righteous Father" in John 17:25. Obviously, because of God's righteous character, He is as Paul said in Titus 1:2 "God; who cannot lie." And God who cannot lie gave the Holy Ghost to the prophets of old as well as to the writers of the New Testament to inspire them to write God's truth and nothing but God's truth. In fact, in John 14:26, the Comforter is identified as the "Spirit of truth, which proceedeth from the Father."

It follows then that whatever writings were inspired by God would be true; there simply cannot be error in any prophecy written by men who were moved by the power of the Holy Ghost. "For the prophecy came not in old time by the will of man: but holy men of God spake as they were moved by the Holy Ghost" (2 Peter 1:21). God gives us a specific test in the Bible so we can test anyone who claims to be a prophet of the only true God. In Deuteronomy 18:20–22, we read,

> But the prophet, which shall presume to speak a word in my name, which I have not commanded him to speak, or that shall speak in the name of other gods, even that prophet shall die. And if thou say in thine heart, How shall we know the word which the LORD hath not spoken? When a prophet speaketh in the name of the LORD, if the thing follow not, nor come to pass, that is the thing which the LORD hath not spoken, but the prophet hath spoken it presumptuously: thou shalt not be afraid of him.

In this way, we can learn who has spoken the truth about God, the prophet Isaiah, or the prophet Joseph Smith.

PROPHESIES OF ISAIAH

The book of Isaiah contains many prophecies, but we will focus on his prophecies concerning Christ. The prophecy and the fulfillment are as follows.

Prophecy	Subject of Prophecy	Fulfillment
Isaiah 7:14	To be born of a virgin	Matthew 1:8–2:1
Isaiah 11:1	Descended from Jesse	Acts 13:22–13
Isaiah 11:2	Anointed by the Spirit	John 1:32
Isaiah 11:3	Quick of understanding and does not judge by appearances	Luke 5:22
Isaiah 42:2–3	Would be very gentle	Matthew 12:14–20
Isaiah 53:3	Despised, rejected, acquainted with grief	Matthew 27:30–31
Isaiah 53:4	Carried our sorrows	Matthew 8:17

Prophecy	Subject of Prophecy	Fulfillment
Isaiah 53:4	Esteemed Him smitten of God	Matthew 27:43
Isaiah 53:5	Wounded for us	Romans 4:25
Isaiah 53:6	Lord laid on Christ our iniquity	Romans 5:8
Isaiah 53:7–8	Opened not His mouth in His own defense	Acts 8:32–35
Isaiah 53:9	With the rich in His death	Matthew 27:57–60
Isaiah 53:11	Travail of soul	Matthew 27:46
Isaiah 53:11	Shall justify many	2 Corinthians 5:19–21
Isaiah 53:12	Numbered with transgressors	Mark 15:24–28
Isaiah 53:12	Made intercession for the transgressors	I John 2:1–2
Isaiah 25:8	Resurrection	Matthew 28; Mark 16; Luke 24; John 20

Isaiah made these prophecies about seven hundred years before the birth of Christ, and each one was fulfilled completely by Jesus Christ of Nazareth. It would be virtually impossible for anyone to make such prophecies without the inspiration of God. According to Deuteronomy 18:20–22, had only one of Isaiah's prophecies failed to be fulfilled, he would have been regarded as a false prophet.

PROPHESIES OF JOSEPH SMITH

The prophecies of Joseph Smith do not fare as well as those of Isaiah. Let's examine five of his prophecies.

Section 84 of the *Doctrine and Covenants* contains a prophecy that both a temple and a city called the New Jerusalem would be built in the State of Missouri. The first five verses read as follows.

A revelation of Jesus Christ unto his servant Joseph Smith, Jun., and six elders, as they united their hearts and lifted their voices on high. Yea, the word of the Lord concerning his church, established in the last days for the restoration of his people, as he has spoken by the mouth of his prophets, and for the gathering of his saints to stand upon Mount Zion, which shall be the city of New Jerusalem. Which city shall be built, beginning at the temple lot, which is appointed by the finger of the Lord, in the western boundaries of the State of Missouri, and dedicated by the hand of Joseph Smith, Jun., and others with whom the Lord was well pleased. Verily this is the word of the Lord, that the city New Jerusalem shall be built by the gathering of the saints, beginning at this place, even the place of the temple, *which temple shall be reared in this generation. For verily this generation shall not pass away until an house shall be built unto the Lord, and a cloud shall rest upon it, which cloud shall be even the glory of the Lord, which shall fill the house.*[1] (emphasis added)

The time of the prophecy was September 22–23, 1832. It is specifically stated that the revelation was of Jesus Christ. A temple and a city were to be built. The place was specified as the temple lot in the western boundaries of the State of Missouri. It is stated that the temple would be reared in this (1832) generation. It is further stated that this (1832) generation would not all pass away until a house would be built unto the Lord. It has been over 180 years since the prophecy was stated. That generation of people have all passed away, and neither the temple nor the city was built. The prophecy failed.

In Section 124:56–60 of the *Doctrine and Covenants*, Joseph Smith prophesied that Nauvoo House would belong to his descendants forever.

And now I say unto you, as pertaining to my boarding house which I have commanded you build for the boarding of strangers, let it be built unto my name, and let my name be named upon it, and let my servant Joseph and his house have place therein, from generation to generation. For this anointing have I put upon his head, that his blessing shall also be put upon the head of his posterity after him. And as I said unto Abraham concerning the kindreds of the earth, even so I say unto my servant Joseph: In thee and thy seed the kindred of the earth be blessed. *Therefore, let my servant Joseph and his seed after him have place in that house, from generation to generation, forever and ever, saith the Lord. And let the name of that house be called Nauvoo House; and let it be a delightful habitation for man.*[2] (emphasis added)

In 1844, Joseph Smith was killed and the Mormon people were driven out of Nauvoo. Joseph Smith and his family no longer owned the house. This prophecy also failed.

While in Kirtland, Ohio, Joseph Smith prophesied that Zion would never be moved out of its place. The prophecy was made on August 2, 1833, and is recorded in the *Doctrine and Covenants* Section 97. Verse 21 gives this definition of Zion: "Therefore, verily, thus saith the Lord, let Zion rejoice, for this is Zion—THE PURE IN HEART; therefore, let Zion rejoice while all the wicked shall mourn."[3]

The preface to the section says that the section "deals particularly with the affairs of the Saints in Zion, Jackson County, Missouri." Verses 19–20 tell us that Zion would never be moved out of its place.

> And the nations of the earth shall honor her, and shall say: Surely Zion is the city of our God, and surely Zion cannot fail, neither be moved out of her place, for God is there and the hand of the Lord is there. And he hath sworn by the power of his might to be her salvation and her high tower.[4]

The nations of the earth have never made such statements about the saints in Jackson County, Missouri. Neither did Zion remain in

Missouri; it moved to Utah. The prophecy is inaccurate and could not have been spoken under the inspiration of the only true God.

Section 87 of the *Doctrine and Covenants* is a prophecy about the Civil War. It is a many-faceted prophecy, and the various aspects of the prophecy are listed below.[5]

Verses (D and C section 87)	Prophecy	Fulfillment
1	War beginning in South Carolina	War began April 12, 1861, in South Carolina
2	Death and misery of many souls	The Civil War
2	War poured out upon all nations	None
3	Southern states divided against Northern states	The Civil War
3	Southern states call on other nations	Called on France and England for national recognition but were refused
3	Those nations shall call on other nations	None
3	They shall call on other nations for the purpose of defending themselves against other nations	None
3	War to be poured out upon all nations beginning in South Carolina	None
4	Slaves marshaled for war	Some were
6	Inhabitants of the earth shall mourn	Only the United States was involved

Verses (D and C section 87)	Prophecy	Fulfillment
6	Famine, plague, earthquake, thunder, lightning as a worldwide judgment	None
6	Will make a full end of all nations	None

For several decades before the Civil War broke out in South Carolina, there was a lot of bickering between the South and the North. South Carolina was the most adamant about seceding from the nation. Any political observer could have predicted what state the war would begin in with some degree of accuracy. Expecting slaves to be involved would be an even easier thing to predict. The only part of the prophecy that could not have been ascertained from the knowledge of the day was the South calling on other nations for recognition. The prophecy completely failed on at least six points.

There is also a prophecy in 2 Nephi 3 that we should examine. Verse 14 tells of a seer the Lord would bless and those who tried to destroy him would be confounded.

> And thus prophesied Joseph, saying: "Behold, that seer will the Lord bless; and they that seek to destroy him shall be confounded; for this promise which I have obtained of the Lord, of the fruit of my loins, shall be fulfilled. Behold, I am sure of the fulfilling of the promise."[6]

The first phrase of verse 14 identifies the one making the prophecy as "Joseph." Verse 15 identifies the seer as Joseph Smith Jun. "And his name shall be called after me; and it shall be after the name of his father." It is apparent that the prophecy is by Joseph Smith Jun. However, those who sought to destroy him were not confounded as predicted. Joseph Smith Jun. was killed by his enemies at Carthage, Illinois, on June 27, 1844. Regardless of who made the prediction, the prophecy could not have been made under the guidance of the only true God, who cannot lie. Deuteronomy 18:20–22 says that if the prophecy does not come to pass, the prophet has spoken it presumptuously and we should not be afraid of him.

At this point, advice in James 1:16–17 is helpful: "Do not err, my beloved brethren. Every good gift and every perfect gift is from above, and cometh down from the Father of lights, with whom is no variableness, neither shadow of turning." Whatever gift of prophecy the prophet Joseph Smith may have had, it certainly was not a perfect gift. Every perfect gift comes down from the Father of lights.

Joseph Smith's gift of prophecy did not come from the only true God. I believe that if I were to put my trust in the prophecies and teachings of Joseph Smith, I would be doing the very thing the Bible warns us about: "Do not err, my beloved brethren."

Perhaps you are saying, "But Wade, you're not being fair. You make it all sound so bad, and it just isn't like that." I understand how you feel. To me, the Church of Jesus Christ of Latter-Day Saints was the very epitome of everything good and righteous. Everything I knew about God and hoped for in the eternal future was bound up in the Mormon Church. I knew nothing else and had no other religious hope. When I began to learn of the problems with Mormon teaching and with Joseph Smith, I was devastated. I refused to acknowledge them. I became angry. I tried to explain them away. I didn't want my beloved prophet to be anything other than what I believed him to be—a true prophet of God.

My parents taught me to believe in the Almighty, the only true God. My primary school teachers taught me likewise. Eventually, I had to realize that the reason I believed Joseph Smith was a true prophet of God was not because of the things he taught but because I had assumed he, Joseph Smith, had believed in the same God I did, the only true God of the Bible. I am sure many Mormon people made and make the same assumption I did. I did not want to leave the Mormon Church, and I desperately clung to the hope that if I studied long and hard enough, I would eventually find that Joseph Smith really believed in the same God I did. But the longer I studied, the more convinced I became that we were very far apart. One of us simply had to be wrong.

At one point, I became so weary of my internal struggles that I decided just to go back to the Mormon Church and accept everything it taught. I was so sick of my doubts and my efforts to resolve them. At the very first sacrament meeting I attended after deciding to return, the speaker spoke on the subject of men being gods in embryo and progressing to godhood. As determined as I was to accept everything without question, I simply could not accept that doctrine. I thought that it was so contrary to what the Bible taught that it could not be right. I prayed, "Dear God, if you want me to leave the Mormon Church, I will. If you want me to stay in the Mormon Church, I will. I just want the truth."

Millions of people grow up sincerely believing something they are sure is the truth. They find later that what they sincerely believed to be true was not true at all. It is not an experience foreign to humankind. Most of us experience it sometime whether in regard to religious faith or something else. I grew up believing with all my heart that the Mormon Church was true and that Joseph Smith was a true prophet. But all my believing did not change one fact. Joseph Smith's prophecies had failed; he believed and taught that there were many gods, but the Bible makes it clear that the prophet whose prophecies fail is not speaking under the guidance of the only true God. In Joshua 24:14–15, we read,

> Now, therefore, fear the LORD and serve him in sincerity and in truth: and put away the gods which your fathers served on the other side of the flood, and in Egypt; and serve ye the LORD. And if it seem evil unto you to serve the LORD, choose you this day whom ye will serve; whether the gods which your fathers served that were on the other side of the flood, or the gods of the Amorites, in whose land ye dwell: but as for me and my house, we will serve the LORD.

I have chosen to serve the LORD.

CHAPTER 4

THE QUESTION OF AUTHORITY PART I

The Mormon priesthood is held to be the authority on which the Mormon Church exists. Without it, there could be no justification for the claim that the Mormon Church has any right to exist. Therefore, an explanation as to why I left the Mormon Church (and can never return) would be incomplete without addressing the subject of priesthood.

Some Bible passages are used to support the Mormon concept of priesthood, but the Mormon concept of priesthood is vastly different from what is taught in the Bible. Let's examine the biblical concept of priesthood.

BIBLICAL PRIESTHOOD

The primary reason for priests and the priesthood in the Bible was to bring sinful, unworthy people to the holy God. Before Moses, the office of priest was held by the heads of families or tribes. Job offered burnt offerings for his family (Job 1:5). Abraham, Isaac, and Jacob offered sacrifices to atone for their sin and those of their families and servants (Genesis 12:7, 13:18, 26:25, 33:20, 25:1–2). This section may seem rather long, but it is necessary to understand the purpose and structure of priesthood in the Bible.

Melchizedek was a contemporary of Abraham and therefore not a Jew because Abraham was the father of the Jewish people. Melchizedek was a priest and the king of Salem and thus combined kingship and priesthood (Genesis 14:18). The Bible does not record Melchizedek's birth, death, or linage. That is why he is used as a symbol of the priesthood of Christ, who is without beginning or end. Christ is High Priest and King. Hebrews 7:17 says, "For he testifieth, Thou art a priest forever after the order (likeness) of Melchizedek."

Leviticus captures the essence of biblical priesthood. The first seven chapters deal with offerings and sacrifices to God. The first is the burnt offering. Chapter 1 gives the details of what it is for and how it is to be done. It represented total devotion to God and acceptance by Him. It was also a type of Christ's total devotion to God's will and His acceptance with the Father (Leviticus 1:1–17, 6:8–13).

The grain offering was a gift acknowledging God's provision and seeking His continued blessing. The grain offering was to be of unbaked flour, baked loaves, or fresh heads of grain. There was to be no leaven. In the Bible, leaven is often a symbol of sin. Allowing no leaven in the offering typified Christ's sinless character and conduct (Leviticus 2:1–16, 6:14–23).

The peace offering was to be of cattle, sheep, or goats and was for thanks and praise offered in peace and fellowship by a cleansed person (Leviticus 3:1–16, 7:14–20). This foreshadowed Christ's death on the cross, which made peace and fellowship possible between God and humanity.

The sin offering was to take away the defilement and guilt of sin (Leviticus 4:1–35, 6:24–30). This offering also foreshadowed the death of Christ, which took away the guilt and defilement of sin for those willing to trust in and accept His redemptive work for them (2 Corinthians 5:21).

The guilt or trespass offering was needed because sometimes, the sinner owes God and sometimes others as well compensation for the injury of sin (Leviticus 5:14, 6:7, 7:1–10).

After the LORD gave these instructions to Moses, Aaron and his sons were ordained to the priesthood to officiate in all these matters for the people of Israel (chapters 8–9). Everything had to be done perfectly. Sinful humanity was dealing with the holy God. Because God's holiness is absolute, even seemingly inconsequential disobedience must be severely punished. An example of this is in chapter 10, where Nadab and Abihu did not do everything exactly right. They offered strange fire before the Lord; they used a source of fire for the offering other than what God had prescribed. We read of the incident in verses 1–3.

> And Nadab and Abihu, the sons of Aaron, took either of them his censer, and put fire there in, and put incense thereon, and offered strange fire before the LORD, which he commanded them not. And there went out fire from the LORD, and devoured them, and they died before the LORD. Then Moses said unto Aaron, "This is it that the LORD spake, saying, I will be sanctified in them that come nigh me, and before all the people I will be glorified. And Aaron held his peace."

The Lord revealed by this incident how absolutely holy He was and how absolutely intolerant He was of the slightest sin. Sinful humanity simply cannot approach God and live. There must be atonement made first, and it must be exactly as prescribed by God; humanity must trust in and accept God's prescribed method of atonement on humanity's behalf; if not, salvation (safety from the wrath of God) is not possible.

In the church age, God's prescribed method of atonement for the sin of man is His Son Jesus Christ. Christ died on the cross as the ultimate and final sacrifice for humanity. That is why Peter, when addressing the Jewish priests, said of Jesus Christ, "Neither is there salvation in any other: for there is none other name under heaven given among men, whereby we must be saved." Having the priesthood didn't save Nadab and Abihu. All the good works they did, did not save them from the wrath of God even for one little act of disobedience. No matter what we do, we cannot save ourselves from God's wrath. We are all sinners (Romans 3:23). The only genuine hope, the only sure thing, is in what God has already done for us in the ultimate, once-and-for-all sacrifice of Christ. "For God so loved the world, that He gave His only begotten Son, that whosoever believeth in him should not perish, but have everlasting life" (John 3:16).

Leviticus 11–15 provides a long list of sins and bodily conditions that make us unfit to come into the presence of God. This makes us much more aware of our need for atonement. The real highpoint of the book, however, is chapter 16, the Day of Atonement, the one day each year during which atonement was made for the sins of the whole nation.

The presence of God on earth was in the holy of holies in the tabernacle. No man could enter the holy of holies without suffering instant death. Only the high priest could enter once a year after having made proper atonement for his sins and for those of the nation. Aaron was warned not to enter the holy of holies where the ark of the covenant was.

> And the LORD said to Moses, speak unto Aaron thy
> brother, that he come not at all times into the holy place
> within the veil before the mercy seat, which is upon the
> ark; that he die not: for I will appear in the cloud upon
> the mercy seat. (Leviticus 16:2)

Aaron had to offer the prescribed offering for himself and his family first (vv. 5–6). Then he had to take two goats, one for the Lord and one for a scapegoat. He offered the Lord's goat for a sin offering. The scapegoat was to be presented before the Lord alive and then let go into the wilderness (vv. 7–10). After completing the blood sacrifices for himself, he did one for the people of Israel: "Then shall he kill the goat of the sin offering, that is for the people, and bring his blood within the veil, and do with that blood as he did with the blood of the bullock, and sprinkle it upon the mercy seat, and before the mercy seat" (v. 15).

The mercy seat was the meeting place between God and man. The blood had to be sprinkled on the mercy seat to atone for the sins of the people. Aaron was to lay both hands on the head of the scapegoat and confess the sins of the nation over the goat. The goat was then taken far into the wilderness and left, never to return, signifying the removal of the sins of Israel far away.

> And Aaron shall lay both his hands upon the head of
> the live goat, and confess over him all the iniquities of
> the children of Israel, and all their transgressions in all
> their sins, putting them on the head of the goat, and
> shall send him away by the hand of a fit man into the

wilderness: And the goat shall bear upon him all their iniquities unto a land not inhabited: and he shall let go the goat in the wilderness. (vv. 21–22)

This ceremony was done once each year (vv. 29–30).

Leviticus 17 reveals the significance of the blood in the sacrifices: "For the life of the flesh is in the blood: and I have given it unto you upon the altar to make an atonement for your souls: for it is the blood that maketh an atonement for the soul" (v. 11). An atonement is a covering to hide man's sin from the sight of God.

Chapters 18–22 contain a list of morals and ethics to live by as well as special laws for the priests. Chapter 23 gives the seven Jewish festivals: Passover, Unleavened Bread, First Fruits, Feast of Weeks (Pentecost), Feast of Trumpets, Day of Atonement, and Feast of Booths. The significance of each is seen in the following chart.

Jewish Feasts	Meaning for Israel under the Law	Fulfillment for God's People under Grace (the church age)
Passover Leviticus 23:4–5	God's redemption of Israel from bondage in Egypt	Believers in Christ are saved from the bondage to sin, 1 Corinthians 5:7
Unleavened Bread Leviticus 23:6–8	Purification from all leaven (leaven a symbol for sin)	All believers in Christ cleansed from all sin, 1 John 1:9; 1 Corinthians 11:23–26
First Fruits Leviticus 23:9–14	Giving of thanks for the first fruits of the harvest; looking forward to the rest of the harvest	Christ, the first to rise from the dead (permanently) with the promise of resurrection for all who believe in Him, 1 Corinthians 15:20, 22

eks	Giving of thanks for	God's first harvest
:15–23; _ weeks after First Fruits. New Testament name is Pentecost	the first harvest (late spring)	of souls redeemed by faith in Christ, Acts 2:1–4, 41; three thousand saved
Feast of Trumpets Leviticus 23:23–25	Israel gathered and trumpets blown in preparation for the Day of Atonement	Drawing near to God and assembling to stir up love, good works, Hebrews 10:22–25, and the Lord's Supper, 1 Corinthians 11:23–26
Day of Atonement Leviticus 16, 23:26–32	Israel solemnly assembled together for repentance and forgiveness under the Old Testament Law system	Believers in Christ forgiven because of Christ's once and for all atonement, Hebrews 9:1–14, 28
Feast of Booths Leviticus 23:34–43	A celebration of harvest and a remembrance of the tabernacles in which the Jews lived while wandering in the wilderness	All peoples gathered under the rulership of the Messiah, the King, at His second coming, Zechariah 14:16–19; Revelation 20:4–6

Jewish people in all countries still practice these festivals. They understand their significance, but they have rejected the Messiah, who came and fulfilled the law of the Old Testament.

Even the furniture in the tabernacle had significance that was fulfilled in Christ. For example, the lamps mentioned in 24:1–4 represented Christ, the Light of the World (John 8:12). And the showbread of 24:5–9 was a type of Christ as the Bread of Life (John 6:35).

Leviticus clearly shows that the primary reason for the priesthood was to reconcile sinful humanity to holy God. In the Old Testament, the Law consisted of three categories—ceremonial law (the festivals, sacrifices and offerings), moral law (Ten Commandments and all other moral commands of the Lord), and civil law (laws that pertain to the operation of Israel as a nation).

Christ fulfilled all aspects of the Law by living in complete obedience to all of it and then by becoming the ultimate sacrifice for sin that rendered all further sacrifices of animals unnecessary and without redemptive value.

As the population of the nation increased, so did the number of priests that officiated in the tabernacle and later in the temple. But there remained only one high priest; there was need for only one high priest to represent the nation before God on special occasions such as the Day of Atonement.

The office and authority of the high priest changed hands from one man to the next as the life or term of service of each high priest ended. For example, the office of high priest changed hands from Aaron (the first high priest under Mosaic Law) to Eleazar when Aaron died (Numbers 20:28). The office changed hands frequently about the time of Christ, each man serving only a short time. There were no fewer than twenty-eight high priests from the reign of Herod to the destruction of the temple by Titus, a period of 107 years.[1]

Aaron was of the Levite tribe, and only the Levites were privileged to serve as priests. God set that tribe apart for that purpose.

> And the LORD spoke unto Moses, saying, "Bring the tribe of Levi near, and present him before Aaron the priest, that they may minister unto him. And they shall keep his charge, and the charge of the whole congregation before the tabernacle of the congregation, to do the service of the tabernacle." (Numbers 3:5–7)

Not all of the men held the priesthood, only those in the tribe of Levi. (See Numbers 8:14–19.)

Only the descendants of Aaron had the privilege and responsibility of the office of high priest. Korah was a Levite who rebelled against

Moses and Aaron by suggesting they had taken too much power and privilege to themselves. It was not their choice, but God's, and God made that abundantly clear as Korah and his followers were all destroyed by being swallowed by the earth in an earthquake. Others were destroyed by fire from the sanctuary.

So to be high priest, one had to be a direct descendant of Aaron (see Numbers 16). This remained true until Christ came. He descended from the royal line of David. Christ is King and also High Priest: He combined the two offices after the example of Melchizedek, who was a priest and a king.

This priesthood will never again change hands because Christ lives forever. He remains the one and only High Priest forever. The writer of the book of Hebrews explains this very clearly in 7:1–3.

> For this Melchizedek, King of Salem, priest of the Most High God, who met Abraham returning from the slaughter of the kings, and blessed him, to whom also Abraham gave the tenth part of all; first being by interpretation King of righteousness, and after that also King of Salem, which is, King of peace; without father, without mother, without descent, having neither beginning of days, nor end of life; but like unto the Son of God; abideth a priest continually.

In 7:3, we learn that Melchizedek did not have a father, mother, or descendants or beginning of days or end of life. Of course, because he was human, we know he had parents; he was born and he died. The point is that the Bible does not record his beginning or end. Thus, he is a symbol of Christ—without beginning and without end, a priest forever. It follows then that the meaning of the word *order* could not be a lineage or fixed succession as asserted by Mormon doctrine but rather a symbol, i.e., according to the nature of—just like Melchizedek.

The book of Hebrews was dedicated to helping the Hebrew people understand how Christ fulfilled all the Old Testament Law and was a better sacrifice and a better High Priest. He was in the likeness of

Melchizedek in that He was of a different tribe than Aaron, is both a King and High Priest, and is a High Priest forever.

The writer of Hebrews explains,

> If therefore perfection were by the Levitical priesthood (for under it the people received the law), what further need was there that another priest should rise after the order of Melchizedek, and not be called after the order of Aaron? For the priesthood being changed, there is made of necessity a change in the law. For he of whom these things are spoken pertaineth to another tribe, of which no man gave attendance at the altar. (Remember that the priesthood was given to the Levite tribe exclusively but Christ was of the tribe of Judah.) For it is evident that our Lord sprang out of Judah; of which tribe Moses spake nothing concerning priesthood. And it is yet far more evident: for that after the similitude of Melchizedek there ariseth another priest, who is made, not after the law of a carnal commandment, but after the power of an endless life. For he testifieth, Thou art a priest forever after the order (likeness) of Melchizedek. (Hebrews 7:11–17)

> And they truly were many priests, because they were not suffered to continue by reason of death: But this man (Christ), because he continueth ever, hath an unchangeable priesthood. Wherefore he is able also to save them to the uttermost that come unto God by him, seeing he ever liveth to make intercession for them. For such an high priest became us, who is holy, harmless, undefiled, separate from sinners, and made higher than the heavens; Who needeth not daily, as those high priests, to offer up sacrifice, first for his own sins, and then for the people's: for this he did once, when he offered up himself. (Hebrews 7:23–27)

Thus, Christ has fulfilled and put an end to the Aaronic priesthood in that there is

- no longer a need for animal sacrifices,
- no longer a need for human high priests with a priesthood passing from one to another,
- no longer a need for the Levitical line of priests,
- no longer a need for a temple in which God resided, and
- no longer a need for a specially appointed man to officiate between man and God.

Everyone can now come directly to God by placing faith in the finished work of Christ's sacrifice on the cross. He is now our High Priest and Advocate forever.

The apostle John explained the work of Christ, who is now at the right hand of God the Father.

> My little children, these things I write unto you, that ye sin not. And if any man sin, we have an advocate with the Father, Jesus Christ the righteous: and He is the propitiation (a sacrifice that satisfied God's demand for justice) for our sins: and not for ours only, but also for the sins of the whole world. (1 John 2:1–2)

The apostle Paul reminds us,

> For there is one God, and one mediator between God and men, the man Christ Jesus; who gave himself a ransom for all, to be testified in due time. (1 Timothy 2:5–6)

Those who receive Jesus Christ, the Son of the only true God, as their Savior become believer priests who having authority to come before God for mercy, help, and intercession for others (Hebrews 4:14–16). Thus, my priesthood is a royal priesthood that authorizes me to come to God in the authority and name of Jesus Christ, the King of Kings (1 Peter 2:9–10).

This high honor is for men and women who receive the true Christ as their Savior. Without doubt, the primary purpose of the priesthood of the Bible is to bring sinful humanity to the holy and otherwise unapproachable God.

MORMON PRIESTHOOD

The primary purpose of the Mormon priesthood is far different; it is to empower people to become gods through the administration of and obedience to the laws and ordinances of the Mormon gospel. Priesthood is said to be the eternal power and authority by which the plan of creation, redemption, and eventually exaltation function. In short, the priesthood is said to be the power of God that a priest obtained from a god before him in the system of eternal progression.

Man's priesthood is said to be God's power and authority delegated to man. This delegated authority authorized men to do all things necessary to the salvation of man. (See chapter 5 for definitions and discussion on the differences between Mormon and biblical salvation.)

In the Mormon priesthood are two degrees, Aaronic and Melchizedek. The Aaronic includes the Levitical priesthood (*Doctrine and Covenants* Section 107:1).[2] In the Aaronic priesthood are the offices of deacon, teacher, priest, and bishop. A bishop of a ward presides over the Aaronic priesthood in his ward and his local church as well as being the presiding high priest. The offices of the Melchizedek priesthood are elder, seventy, high priest, patriarch or evangelist, and apostle.

The functions and duties of the offices of the Mormon priesthood are summarized as follows.

1. Deacon: Deacons are to watch over the church and to be standing ministers to the church (*Doctrine and Covenants* Section 84:111).[3] They are to assist teachers, warn, expound, exhort, teach, and invite all to come to Christ (*Doctrine and Covenants* Section 20:57–59).[4]

2. Teacher: Teachers are to watch over the church always to be with and strengthen them and to see there is no iniquity in the church, neither hardness with each other, neither lying, backbiting, nor evil speaking. And see that the church meet together often and also see that all the members do their duty. They are to warn, expound, exhort, and teach, and invite all to come to Christ. Plus, they can do all the functions of the deacons (*Doctrine and Covenants* Section 20:53–59).[5]

3. Priest: The duties of the priest are to preach, teach, expound, exhort, baptize, and administer the sacrament. They are to visit in the homes of the members and exhort them to pray and to attend to family duties. They are to lead meetings when no elder is present, and they can ordain deacons and teachers and priests as well as perform the duties of all three (*Doctrine and Covenants* Section 20:46–49).[6]

4. Bishop: The duties of the bishop are to preside over the Aaronic priesthood in his ward, and he is president of the priests' quorum. As such, he deals primarily with temporal matters (*Doctrine and Covenants* Section 107:68).[7] He has the gift of discernment and power to discern all other spiritual gifts (*Doctrine and Covenants* Section 46:27).[8] He is called a common judge in Israel (*Doctrine and Covenants* Section 107:74).[9]

5. Elder: An elder is to administer in spiritual things, teach, preach, expound, exhort, baptize, watch over the church, and perform confirmation by the laying on of hands and giving of the Holy Ghost. He is to conduct meetings, administer to the sick, function in church court, and perform any duty of the lesser priesthood (*Doctrine and Covenants* Section 20:38–45, 46:2, 53:3, 42:12, 43–52, 80).[10]

6. Seventy: A seventy is to act in the name of the Lord in building up the church, regulate all affairs of the church in all nations, and be called upon by the traveling high council for assistance. They are called upon for preaching and administering the gospel (*Doctrine and Covenants* Section 107:34, 38).[11]

7. High Priest: The high priest ministers in spiritual things (*Doctrine and Covenants* Section 107:18).[12] He is to travel and

preach the gospel (*Doctrine and Covenants* Section 84:111).[13]
He is to perfect the saints and do all the things elders, seventies,
or bearers of the Aaronic priesthood can do (*Doctrine and
Covenants* Section 68:19).[14]

8. Patriarch or Evangelist: The major duty of the patriarch is to
give patriarchal blessings to members of the church. But he can
perform any duty of any priesthood office under him (*Doctrine
and Covenants* Section 107: 39, 124:91–94).[15]

9. Apostle: The apostle is to proclaim the Mormon gospel
everywhere and to administer the affairs of the church (*Doctrine
and Covenants* Section 107:58–100).[16]

In all the duties listed for all the offices of both priesthoods in the
Mormon Church, there is no mention whatever of sacrificial atonement
for sin to bring sinful, unworthy man to God. Nor is there mention of
the believers' right to approach God by virtue of the sacrificial blood
atonement of Christ, the High Priest. The emphasis is not on bringing
sinful man to God as is true of the biblical priesthood but rather on
the power and authority to function in their respective positions with
the understanding that holding the priesthood gives them the power
necessary to reach godhood.

Obviously, the priesthood of the Bible and the priesthood of the
Mormon Church, primarily outlined in the *Doctrine and Covenants*,
are vastly different. The chart below will make this even more apparent.

Biblical Priesthood	Mormon Priesthood
Essence: A God-appointed position	Essence: The power of god which he received from his god before him.
Purpose: To officiate in bringing sinful man to God	Purpose: The power of god delegated to man to enable him to fulfill his religious duties and eventually become a god

Biblical Priesthood	Mormon Priesthood
Function: Old Testament Age: officiating in animal sacrifices to provide blood atonement for God's people	Function: Old Testament: with some variations approximately the same as today (according to the Book of Mormon)
Church Age: All of the priesthood is fulfilled in Christ who is now the one and only High Priest forever	Church Age: (from the inception of the Mormon Church) all the various functions listed above for each office in the priesthood
Rights of Each True Believer: Each person who trusts in Christ's ultimate sacrifice for him is a believer priest and as such has the right to enter the presence of God for mercy, help, blessing, praise, and intercession	Rights of Each Priesthood Holder: The right to fulfill his respective duties that help him progress toward godhood

At first glance, it may appear that the Mormon concept of priesthood is the biggest and the best. After all, the Bible promises only access to God while the Mormon priesthood promises one can actually become a god, but all that glitters is not gold. We should ask not which promises the most but which actually delivers the most. Which promise is true?

In chapter 1, we established that the Bible teaches God is one and has existed from all eternity as God, who never changes. We also noted that God declares there are no other gods before Him and there will be none after Him.

In chapter 2, we established the reliability of the Bible as a source of truth noting the providential preservation of the manuscripts and the fulfillment of Bible prophecy, etc. We have noted the utter failure of the Book of Mormon to stand the same tests as the Bible.

In chapter 3, we studied further the prophecy of the Bible centering on the prophecies of Isaiah. We saw the accuracy of Isaiah's prophecies and the failure of Joseph Smith's prophecies. Joseph Smith testified to his own inability to declare and publish the truth by the failure of his prophecies.

I have chosen to rely on the Bible and what God declares about Himself in it. Because of the proven reliability of the Bible, I have chosen to accept the biblical concept of priesthood as the true priesthood. According to the God of the Bible, the gods of Joseph Smith do not exist. Since his gods do not exist, he had no inspiration for his prophecies, and thus they failed. Since his gods do not exist, neither does his priesthood, and the promise of exaltation to godhood is an empty promise.

If the Mormon priesthood does not exist, where is the authority of the Mormon Church of which it so often speaks? Though cherished, it is an empty claim. The claim of the Mormon priesthood to be the power of God is an affront to the true Father in heaven. It makes priesthood greater than God. That is, if the father in heaven, as Smith conceived him to be, had no priesthood, he would not be a god. The true Father in heaven is a self-existent being; He is not dependent on some other source of power to make Him God.

The Mormon concept of priesthood also fails to see the clear-cut distinction between the Old Testament Law age and the New Testament church age. The deacon, bishop, elder, and apostle belong to the church age. The priest, high priest, and patriarch belong to the Old Testament Law system. The seventy is simply the group of disciples Jesus sent out to preach on one occasion (Luke 10:1–17); it does not represent an office. The teacher is not an office but rather a spiritual gift that enables one to teach well. (We will discuss church officers in greater detail in chapter 5.)

When Nadab and Abihu offered strange fire on the altar of God and were consumed by the fire of God, they had deviated only slightly from God's established priesthood. The priesthood of Mormonism deviates greatly from what the only true God has established. Had I continued to accept the priesthood of the Mormon Church, I am convinced that I would have fared no better than Nadab and Abihu on the day of judgment.

CHAPTER 5

——◇——

THE QUESTION OF AUTHORITY PART II

A major premise of the Mormon Church is that an apostasy of the early church occurred when the original apostles passed away. As noted in the last chapter, the Mormon concept of priesthood fails to see the clear-cut distinction between the Old Testament Law age and the New Testament church age. Offices of the Mormon priesthood include offices from both the Old Testament Law dispensation and the New Testament church dispensation. It is a basic belief of the Mormon Church that the church has been in existence since the time of Adam. Actually, the church came into existence only after Christ's crucifixion, resurrection, and ascension; the word *church* does not even appear in the Old Testament.

There are seven distinct periods or dispensations clearly recognizable in the Bible. The first dispensation was that of innocence, which was from the time of creation to the fall of Adam and Eve. Second was the dispensation of conscience, which extended from the fall to the universal flood. The third dispensation was that of human government when God commanded capital punishment for murder. That dispensation extended from the universal flood to Abraham. Abraham began the patriarchal age, which lasted until Moses.

Moses began the Law dispensation that ended with the first advent of Christ. The church age is from the first coming of Christ until the rapture of the church described in 1 Thessalonians 4:13–18. It is the church dispensation or age in which we now live. Following the church age will be the millennial reign of Christ, which will begin at the return of Christ to the earth, and it is the seventh dispensation.

INVALID CLAIM OF EARLY CHURCH APOSTASY

Even if one does not believe that the seven dispensations are distinctive enough to be recognized and set apart, to haphazardly lump the Old Testament era and the church age together will result in gross misrepresentations of the meaning of the Bible. The belief is that when the original apostles died, the church and its authority were taken from the earth necessitating a restoration of the church through Joseph Smith. Scripture passages from the Old and New Testaments are used to support the claim. One such passage is Matthew 24:9–11.

> Then shall they deliver you up to be afflicted, and shall kill you: and ye shall be hated of all nations for my name's sake. And then shall many be offended, and shall betray one another, and shall hate one another. And many false prophets shall rise, and shall deceive many.

This is not talking about an apostasy of the newly established church but rather conditions on earth just prior to the second coming of Christ at the end of the age. (See Matthew 24:1–3 to get the whole context.)

Another passage used to teach that the early church apostatized and was taken from the earth is Mark 12:1–9, the parable of the vineyard; in it, the Lord Jesus told of how those in charge of the vineyard would treat Him. In Psalm 80:8, we are told the vineyard was brought up out of Egypt: "Thou hast brought a vine out of Egypt: thou hast cast out the heathen, and planted it." Isaiah 5:2–7 clearly states the symbolism of a vineyard being Israel and especially verse 7: "For the vineyard of the LORD of hosts *is* the house of Israel, and the men of Judah his pleasant plant: and he looked for judgment, but behold oppression; for righteousness, but behold a cry." Thus, in Mark 12:1–9, Jesus is not talking about any apostasy of the church but about Israel's rejection of Him.

Acts 20:28–30 is also used to support the Mormon teaching that the early church apostatized.

> Take heed therefore unto yourselves, and to all the flock, over which the Holy Ghost hath made you overseers, to feed the church of God, which he hath purchased with his own blood. For I know this, that after my departing shall grievous wolves enter in among you, not sparing the flock. Also, of your own selves shall men arise, speaking perverse things, to draw away disciples after them.

That sounds pretty bad, doesn't it? But read on through verse 32.

> Therefore watch, and remember, that by the space of three years I ceased not to warn every one night and day with tears. And now, brethren, I commend you to God, and to the word of his grace, which is able to build you up, and to give you an inheritance among all them which are sanctified.

Some people will apostatize, but God is able to strengthen His people and preserve them.

Other passages taken out of context and used to teach the apostasy of the early church include Galatians 1:6–9, which addresses false teaching only in Galatia; 2 Thessalonians 2:1–12, which addresses the future time when the Antichrist will be revealed, not the beginning of the church; 1 Timothy 4:1–3, which warns of some but not all departing from the faith; and 2 Timothy 4:3–4, which warns of those who would oppose the gospel, but there is no indication of apostasy of the whole church. In fact, Paul exhorted Timothy to continue and make full proof of his ministry. In 2 Peter 2:1–2, we read warnings of false teachers, but in verse 9, we learn, "The Lord knoweth how to deliver the godly out of temptations, and to reserve the unjust unto the day of judgment to be punished."

Finally, Amos 8:11–12 is sometimes used to teach the apostasy of the early church after the death of the apostles, but it is a warning to Israel of its impending captivity because of its sin. Read the full context of the passage and let it speak for itself.

The Mormon teaching is, however, that after Christ came personally to earth, ministered to Israel, was crucified for humanity's sin, rose from the grave, and established His church, the whole effort fizzled and died within sixty years. After that, it was another 1,700 years before He attempted to put His church back on earth through Joseph Smith. The idea suggests that Satan has power to thwart God, that he could stop the work of God on earth for 1,700 years. Such a claim I cannot accept. It has never been demonstrated to me that Satan has such powers or that God is so impotent.

The doctrine that Christ's church had to be restored to the earth is based on three misconceptions—that the church was taken from the earth at the death of the apostles, that the only true church must be organized with apostles in authority and leadership as was the early New Testament church, and that the transmission of God's authority is first from God to man and then from man to man by the laying on of hands by those who are in authority.

CONTINUITY OF THE CHURCH

It was not God's intention to allow the church to be taken from the earth after its inception. In Matthew 16:18, Jesus said, "I will build My church and the gates of hell shall not prevail against it." The word *hell* is translated from the Greek Hades, which means the place of the dead. Jesus was saying that nothing, not even death, could stop Him from building His church. That would certainly include the death of the apostles.

The apostles were foundational to the church. A foundation does not extend up through the walls to the roof of the building; a foundation is the solid base on which the remainder of the building rests. The apostles were intended to be foundational to the church, not to continue as the rest of the church was built throughout the age. Paul explained this to the Ephesian Christians in Ephesians 2:19–22.

> Now ye are no more strangers and foreigners, but
> fellow citizens with the saints, and of the household
> of God; and are built upon the foundation of the
> apostles and prophets, Jesus Christ himself being the
> chief cornerstone; in whom all the building fitly framed
> together groweth unto an holy temple in the Lord: in
> whom ye also are builded together for an habitation of
> God through the Spirit.

God's people are the building, "a holy temple in the Lord." The apostles, prophets, and Christ were foundational (Ephesians 2:20). Christ is also said to be the head of the church in Colossians 1:18. The apostles were never spoken of as being at the head of the church; they are foundational only.

The fact that God never intended for the apostles to serve throughout the church age is also seen in that the twelve apostles never ordained other apostles. Judas Iscariot was replaced because he betrayed the Lord and was lost, but the faithful apostles were never replaced. For example, James was martyred when the church was only a few years old, but he was never replaced (Acts 12:1–2).

Yes, there have been periods of apostasy during the past two thousand years of church history, and there is some today, but the apostasy has never been universal. God has always had His faithful ones to carry on His work.

The Mormon Church depends on apostolic succession to transmit church authority. The fact is that God never intended for apostolic succession. The office of apostle is a very exclusive office. The apostles were chosen directly by the Lord and given miraculous gifts by Him to attest to their divine appointment.

> And when he had called his twelve disciples, he gave
> them power against unclean spirits, to cast them out
> and to heal all manner of disease. Now the names of the
> apostles are these; The first, Simon, who is called Peter,
> and Andrew his brother; James the son of Zebedee, and

John his brother; Phillip, and Bartholomew; Thomas, and Matthew the publican; James, the son of Alphaeus, Lebbaeus, whose surname was Thaddaeus; Simon the Canaanite, and Judas Iscariot, who also betrayed him. (Matthew 10:1–4)

There is a special relationship between the apostles and the nation of Israel. Their future assignment in the kingdom of heaven will be to sit as judges over the twelve tribes of Israel.

Then answered Peter and said unto him, Behold, we have forsaken all, and followed thee; what shall we have therefore? And Jesus said unto them, "Verily I say unto you, that ye which have followed me, in the regeneration when the Son of man shall sit in the throne of his glory, ye also shall sit upon twelve thrones, judging the twelve tribes of Israel." (Matthew 19:27–28)

After Israel rejected Christ, the apostles became foundation stones for the church; they received the Holy Ghost and preached the gospel to Jews and Gentiles.

There was one last indispensable qualification for being an apostle—the person had to have been with Jesus from the beginning of His ministry all the way through to His ascension, being an eyewitness of the resurrection. Matthias met this requirement.

Wherefore these men which have companied with us all the time that the Lord Jesus went in and out among us, beginning from the baptism of John, unto that same day that he was taken up from us, must one be ordained to be a witness with us of his resurrection. (Acts 1:21–22)

All these qualifications make the office of apostle most exclusive. Even if someone today would claim to have seen the risen Lord in a vision, he could not claim to have accompanied the Lord Jesus from the baptism of John until the ascension, nor could he take his place as one of the judges of the twelve tribes of Israel. There are only twelve tribes and only twelve thrones of judgment, and they are all taken.

In addition to this, there will be twelve foundation stones under the wall of the New Jerusalem. Each one will have a name of one of the apostles: "And the wall of the city had twelve foundations, and in them the name of the twelve apostles of the Lamb" (Revelation 21:14). There are only twelve foundations, and they are all taken.

The apostle Paul was called by the Lord for the special purpose of taking the gospel to the Gentiles. He was not of the twelve. He was an eyewitness of the risen Lord, but he did not accompany Christ from the first as did Mathias. He will not serve as a judge over one of the tribes of Israel in the kingdom age. Perhaps that is why he called himself "the least of the apostles" (1 Corinthians 19:9).

Paul did not lack God's authority; he was chosen personally by Christ for an exclusive task and was not one of the twelve. It is unquestionable that apostolic succession was never intended by the Lord. So how then did the church continue without apostles? We must first understand what the church is.

THE ONLY TRUE CHURCH

The word *church* in the New Testament is translated from the Greek *ekklesia*, which means an assembly.[1] The word was used to designate the assembly of people who had obtained the mercy of God through faith in Christ. One who has obtained the mercy of God is spared the wrath of God for sin; he has received mercy rather than justice and thus is saved. The biblical meaning of the words *saved* or *salvation* is a place of safety. To obtain salvation is to reach a place of safety from the wrath of God against sin. Grace is the special and undeserved favor of God toward us. Ephesians 2:8–9 explains, "For by grace are ye saved through faith; and that not of yourselves: it is the gift of God: not of works, lest any man should boast."

God's special kindness is extended toward us by faith in Christ. "By grace are ye saved through faith." "It is the gift of God." Peter spoke of those who were redeemed by the blood of Christ and had their faith and hope in Him.

Forasmuch as ye know that ye were not redeemed with corruptible things, as silver and gold, from your vain conversation received by tradition from your fathers; but with the precious blood of Christ, as of a lamb without blemish and without spot: who verily was foreordained before the foundation of the world, but was manifest in these last times for you, who by him do believe in God, that raised him up from the dead, and gave him glory; that your faith and hope might be in God. (1 Peter 1:18–21)

He also said of the redeemed,

Ye also, as lively stones, are built up a spiritual house, an holy priesthood, to offer up spiritual sacrifices acceptable to God by Jesus Christ. (1 Peter 2:5)

Then he described the redeemed as a chosen generation, who are now the people of God and who have obtained mercy.

But ye are a chosen generation, a royal priesthood, an holy nation, a peculiar people; that ye should shew forth the praises of Him who hath called you out of darkness into his marvelous light: which in time past were not a people, but are now the people of God: which had not obtained mercy, but now have obtained mercy. (1 Peter 2:9–11)

Titus 3:4–7 further explains this mercy and its result.

But after that the kindness and love of God our Savior toward man appeared, not by works of righteousness which we have done, but according to his mercy he saved us, by the washing of regeneration, and the renewing of the Holy Ghost; which he shed on us abundantly through Jesus Christ our Savior; that being justified by his grace, we should be made heirs according to the hope of eternal life.

In 2 Timothy 1:9, we read,

> ... who hath saved us, and called us with an holy calling, not according to our works, but according to his own purpose and grace, which was given us in Christ Jesus before the world began.

Notice that the word *saved* is in the past tense. "Not hoping to be saved, nor working to get saved by works of righteousness, but according to his mercy he saved us," Paul said to Titus (Titus 3:5; see also Luke 7:50; 1 Corinthians 1:18; 2 Corinthians 2:15).

The only true church is made up of every person who is saved from God's wrath through faith in Christ regardless of what organized church they belong to or do not belong to. It is not the organized church that saves us from the wrath of God; it is faith in the Savior. Jesus made that so clear in John 3:17–18.

> For God sent not his Son into the world to condemn the world; but that the world through him might be saved. *He that believeth on him is not condemned: but he that believeth not is condemned already*, because he hath not believed in the name of the only begotten Son of God. (emphasis added)

The Mormon definition of salvation is twofold. First, there is a general salvation referred to as resurrection. Everyone except for a very few sons of perdition perhaps is exempt from agony in hell. Second, exaltation results from living of the laws and ordinances of the Mormon gospel and enables one to attain the celestial kingdom, which would include becoming a god. Damnation is not eternal punishment in a burning hell as Christ taught but rather the knowledge that one could have attained a higher kingdom but did not according to Mormon teaching.

The general salvation taught by Mormonism simply cannot be true.

Jesus said in Matthew 7:13–14, "Enter ye in at the strait gate: for wide is the gate, and broad is the way, that leadeth to destruction, and many there be which go in there at: because strait is the gate, and narrow is the way, which leadeth unto life, and few there be that find it." There are many who go to destruction. Certainly, destruction could not be salvation. Few enter life, not the vast majority.

The apostle John wrote of the future judgment of those who had not obtained mercy.

> And I saw a great white throne, and him that sat on it from whose face the earth and heaven fled away; and there was found no place for them. And I saw the dead, small and great, stand before God; and the books were opened; and another book was opened, which is the book of life: and the dead were judged out of those things which were written in the books, according to their works. And the sea gave up the dead which were in it; and death and hell delivered up the dead which were in them: and they were judged every man according to their works. And death and hell were cast into the lake of fire. This is the second death. And whosoever was not found written in the book of life was cast into the lake of fire. (Revelation 20:11–15)

All who receive the mark of the beast during the reign of the Antichrist will suffer unending torment.

> And the third angel followed them, saying with a loud voice, if any man worship the beast and his image, and receive his mark in his forehead, or in his hand, the same shall drink of the wine of the wrath of God, which is poured out without mixture into the cup of his indignation; and he shall be tormented with fire and brimstone in the presence of the holy angels, and in the presence of the Lamb. And the smoke of their torment ascendeth up forever and ever: and they whosoever receiveth the mark of his name. (Revelation 14:9–11)

The reason people who have not come to God to ask forgiveness through faith in Christ are punished eternally is that their sin has not been forgiven them and they remain guilty forever. There is nothing they can do to get free from their guilt if they have rejected God and have neglected God's gift of forgiveness offered in Christ. Only those whose names are written in the Lamb's Book of Life will be spared eternal punishment for their sin.

As already stated, Jesus makes it certain that the majority will go to destruction. True salvation is not automatic; there is a choice to be made; there must be repentance. Faith must be exercised: "Therefore being justified by faith, we have peace with God through our Lord Jesus Christ" (Romans 5:1). If everyone is automatically saved simply because Christ died for the sins of the world and rose to life, why does the Bible emphasize the need to exercise faith? "We are saved by grace through faith," "Being justified by faith," etc. No one is forgiven just because Christ paid for all sin.

Again, John 3:18 tells us, "He that believeth not is condemned already, because he hath not believed in the name of the only begotten Son of God." Verse 36 says, "He that believeth not shall not see life, but the wrath of God abideth on him."

Again, true salvation from God's wrath is not automatic. One must ask God's forgiveness and trust in the shed blood of Christ for atonement for sin: "Whosoever shall call upon the name of the Lord shall be saved" (Romans 10:13). Good works won't help; they cannot buy God's forgiveness. Only the blood of Christ can do that. Good works mean nothing until a person has obtained God's mercy through faith in the blood of Christ. Then and only then will good works be rewarded.

> Not everyone that saith unto me, Lord, Lord, shall enter into the kingdom of heaven; but he that doeth the will of my Father which is in heaven. Many will say to me in that day, Lord, Lord, have we not prophesied in thy name? and in thy name have cast out devils? and in thy name done many wonderful works? And then will I profess unto them, I never knew you: depart from me, ye that work iniquity. (Matthew 7:21–23)

Good works, even miraculous works, are regarded by God as "iniquity" if a person has not repented and trusted in Christ for forgiveness of their sins.

This is the true church. Every person who has obtained God's mercy by being justified by faith is a member of Christ's body. The apostle Paul wrote to the church in Ephesus addressing them as saints "who are the faithful in Christ" (Ephesians 1:1). He said several things about them in the first several verses.

> Blessed be the God and Father of Our Lord Jesus Christ, who hath blessed us with all spiritual blessings in heavenly places in Christ; according as he hath chosen us in him before the foundation of the world, that we would be holy and without blame before him in love: Having predestinated us unto the adoption of children by Jesus Christ to himself, according to the good pleasure of his will, to the praise of the glory of his grace, wherein he hath made us accepted in the Beloved. In whom we have redemption through his blood, the forgiveness of sins, according to the riches of his grace. (Ephesians 1:3–7)

Notice in verse 7 that he said, "We [himself and the Ephesian saints] have redemption through his blood, the forgiveness of sins according to the riches of his grace." In verses 22–23 of the same chapter, we learn that the church is called the body of Christ: "And hath put all things under his feet, the fullness of him to be head over all things to the church, which is his body, the fullness of him that filleth all in all."

In Paul's first letter to the Corinthians, he called the Christians at Corinth "the church of God, them that are sanctified in Christ, called to be saints, those that call upon the name of Jesus Christ." In 1 Corinthians 6:9–11, he said to them,

> Know ye not that the unrighteous shall not inherit the kingdom of God? Be not deceived: neither fornicators, nor idolaters, nor adulterers, nor effeminate, nor abusers

of themselves with mankind, nor thieves, nor covetous, nor drunkards, nor revilers, nor extortioners, shall inherit the kingdom of God. And such were some of you: but ye are washed, but ye are sanctified, but ye are justified in the name of the Lord Jesus, and by the Spirit of our God.

In 1 Corinthians 12: 27, he said to them, "Now ye are the body of Christ and members in particular."

You see, it's those who are justified by faith, saved, redeemed, cleansed of sin, and have obtained mercy who are members of the body of Christ, the church. With regard to salvation from sin and the gift of eternal life, it makes no difference what religious denomination a person belongs to or does not belong to. It is not the outward church organization that God uses to judge whether someone belongs to Him. It is not denominational membership or lack thereof that God uses to judge who belongs to Him. Only those who have been cleansed of sin belong to God. Men tend to look on the outward appearance, but God looks on the heart (1 Samuel 16:7).

This was a great problem for me when I began to discover the serious problems in the teachings of the prophet Joseph Smith. My question was, if the Mormon Church was not the true church, which one was? When I discovered that every person who believed in the only true God and trusted in Jesus Christ as his or her Savior is cleansed from sin, and when I discovered that every person thus cleansed from sin is a member of Christ's body, His church, what a glorious light of understanding shined into my life!

God is not fooled by all the outward efforts of man to appear righteous; His understanding is infinite (Psalm 147:5). God is not impressed with religious organizations that are small (Mormon Church membership is a few million) or large (Catholic Church membership is nearly 900 million). He has no need of temples made with hands (Acts 17:24–27). But God does seek those who will worship Him in spirit and in truth: "But the hour cometh and now is, when the true worshipers shall worship the Father in spirit and in truth: for the Father seeketh such to worship him. God is a Spirit: and they that worship him must worship in spirit and in truth" (John 4:23–24).

I repeat—those who believe in the only true God and receive and trust in His only Son Jesus Christ as their own Savior is cleansed by the blood of Christ, have obtained mercy, and are members of His body, the only true church. Jesus said, "All that the Father giveth me shall come to me; and him that cometh to me I will in no wise cast out" (John 6:37).

No one has to come to God through an organized church. In fact, that is impossible. Jesus said emphatically, "I am the way, the truth, and the life, no man cometh unto the Father but by me" (John 14:6). Church organization has its place and is very important, but to insist that true salvation can be had only through one particular church is at best a perversion of what Jesus said about Himself being the only way to God. At worst, it is a dangerous teaching that leads people away from a simple faith in Christ, who is the only way to be saved from the wrath of God.

Joseph Smith said that the Lord had told him that all religious organizations were "all wrong," and "all their creeds were an abomination," and that "those professors were all corrupt."[2] That statement precludes the possibility of any and all religious organizations except the Mormon Church being in God's will. I believe that such a conclusion cannot be supported when religious organizations are compared with the Bible. It is true that some have corrupted their doctrines and teaching, but many are in harmony with the Bible and are used by the Lord in His program of winning people to Himself.

Joseph Smith's statement focuses entirely on religious organization and ignores the fact that there were true believers in those organizations he condemned. That results in a subtle deception, an inability to see beyond the religious organization to identify the living body of born-again believers.

Christ's church is not an organization; it is a living organism consisting of all persons who are saved by faith in the true God and in the blood of Christ shed to pay for their sins.

TRANSMISSION OF AUTHORITY

The body of Christ is manifest on the local level by the local churches, which are assemblies of saved people. Organization was developed in the New Testament for local churches. In the New Testament church, elders were appointed in every church to govern and oversee the local body. A church hierarchy that would rule over all local churches was not intended. If you are of Mormon background, this may sound strange to you because we have been taught that the transmission of authority is from God to man and then from one man to another by the laying on of hands by those who are in authority. We were also taught that authority could not be transmitted in any other way.

The laying on of hands was employed in the early church in three ways: for the reception of the Holy Ghost after belief in Christ, for appointment to church office, and for healing.

At times, the gift of the Holy Ghost was received without the laying on of hands. The first example is that of the apostles themselves in Acts 2:1–4, and following that, three thousand were saved on the Day of Pentecost (Acts 2:41–47). When Philip preached to the Ethiopian and he believed and was baptized, the Spirit immediately caught Philip away and he did not lay hands on the man to receive the Holy Ghost (Acts 8:37–40). Saul received the Holy Ghost by the laying on of Ananias's hands before baptism, the reverse of other occasions (Acts 9:17–19; compare Acts 8:14–17).

When Peter preached the gospel to Cornelius and his household, the Holy Ghost fell on them without the laying on of hands even though Peter was there in person and could have done so. They received the Holy Ghost and spoke in tongues even before being baptized (Acts 10:34–48).

When Peter commanded the healing of Aeneas in the name of Christ (Acts 9:32–35), he did not use the laying on of hands. Peter, in the authority of Christ, commanded Tabitha, who had died, to arise. She rose from the dead and sat up without the laying on of hands. Peter took her by the hand after she was alive and helped her stand (Acts 9:36–43).

Acts 14:8–10 records Paul's healing of a man crippled from birth, and we also notice the Lord Jesus doing the same thing when the Roman centurion came to Him asking Him to heal his servant. Jesus did not even go to where the servant was but spoke the word only (Matthew 8:5–10).

Nowhere in the biblical record of Christ's ordination of the twelve is there mention of His laying His hands on them (Matthew 10:1–7;

Mark 3:13–19; Luke 6:13–16). Jesus did breathe on the disciples after He rose from the dead.

> And when he had so said, he shewed unto them his hands and his side. Then were the disciples glad, when they saw the Lord. Then said Jesus to them again, Peace be unto you: as my Father hath sent me, even so send I you. And when he had said this, he breathed on them, and saith unto them, Receive ye the Holy Ghost. (John 20:20–22)

However, that was not laying on of hands, which is insisted upon by Mormon teaching to transmit authority.

When Matthias was chosen to replace Judas Iscariot, there was no evidence of the use of the laying on of hands; rather, they cast lots (Acts 1:22–26). In Acts 13:1–4, Barnabas and Saul were first called by the Holy Ghost. Then the church set them apart for their special work by laying hands on them. There is no indication that the act of laying on of hands in any way gave them more power or authority to complete the task. Verse 4 clearly states that they were sent forth by the Holy Ghost.

In Acts 14:23, we are told that Paul and Barnabas "ordained them elders in every church." The Greek word for ordain is *cheirotoneo*, which means to appoint or install. In other places, it means to elect by raising the hand.[3] Paul and Barnabas may or may not have used the laying on of hands.

Many passages depict the use of the laying on of hands in healings, confirming the Holy Ghost, and ordinations. Generally speaking, laying on of hands is used as an outward sign of man's recognition and approval of what God has or is sovereignly bestowing.

It is entirely right to practice the laying on of hands as used in the Bible, but to make it a hard and fast rule insisting that true authority simply cannot be transmitted to man without it is a gross error; the Bible does not support it. Making the laying on of hands a rule to transmit authority contributes to the error that the Mormon Church is the only one that has proper authority.

How then is God's authority transmitted to His people for service and leadership in the church age? We have already discussed biblical priesthood and learned that when people trust in Jesus Christ as their Lord and Savior, they become believer priests with authority to come before God for mercy, help, intercession for others, and so on.

Also received by believers are one or more spiritual gifts given to every true believer to enable him or her for service. Paul explained in 1 Corinthians 12:4–11,

> Now there are diversities of gifts, but the same Spirit. And there are diversities of operations, but it is the same God which worketh all in all. But the manifestation of the Spirit is given to every man to profit withal. For to one is given by the same Spirit the word of wisdom; to another the word of knowledge by the same Spirit; to another faith by the same Spirit; to another the gifts of healing by the same Spirit; to another discerning of spirits; to another divers kinds of tongues: but all these worketh that one and the selfsame Spirit, dividing to every man severally as he will.

The Spirit gives gifts to every man—a special personal touch of God on every true believer. The list of gifts given in this passage is partial; other gifts are listed in Romans 12:6–8 and Ephesians 4:11. Some of these gifts were specifically for the founding of the church and are not for today. We have already seen this demonstrated with the gift of apostleship. We will not take time to differentiate between the temporary gifts and the permanent gifts here, but it is clear that the Spirit gives gifts to every believer in the true God and His Son Jesus Christ. That bestowal of gifts is God's personal touch on every true believer, and the authority to exercise those gifts comes with the gifts. These gifts equip each believer to do the ministry God has intended him or her to do. Each gift can be developed further by diligent study and application. For example, the gifts of pastor and teacher may have been given to someone, but that person might not discover the gifts until having experienced such work.

Once discovered, spiritual gifts can be developed just as natural gifts can. In Ephesians 4:11, the gifts of pastor and teacher are a dual gift. That is, teachers might not have the gift of pastor, but pastors must have the gift of teacher because of their task of teaching God's people along with shepherding them. A teacher is one who is gifted in discovering Bible truths and communicating them clearly to others. The gift of pastor is simply the gift of shepherding God's people. He is an overseer of the local church. A bishop (though not one of the spiritual gifts) is an overseer. So we see that a bishop and a pastor are really the same ministry. The term *bishop* describes the position of the overseer, and *pastor* describes the function of an overseer.

Let's assume God has saved a man and has given him the gifts of pastor and teacher. When he begins to realize he has such abilities, he will begin to experience a desire to oversee, shepherd, and teach God's people. Such a desire is good (1 Timothy 3:1). But a person should not be appointed to the office until he is qualified. For example, a person may be gifted at mathematics, but until the person has studied the disciplines of math, principles of mechanical function, and related disciplines, the person is not qualified to be a mechanical engineer. Mastering the disciplines of pastoral ministry, biblical knowledge, and character development is a must for success in ministry. In 1 Timothy 3:1–7, we read the qualifications for a bishop or overseer of God's people.

> This is a true saying, if a man desire the office of a bishop, he desireth a good work. A bishop then must be blameless, the husband of one wife, vigilant, sober, of good behavior, given to hospitality, apt to teach; not given to wine, no striker, not greedy of filthy lucre; but patient, not a brawler, not covetous; one that ruleth well his own house, having his children in subjection with all gravity; (for if a man know not how to rule his own house, how shall he take care of the church of God?), not a novice, lest being lifted up with pride he fall into the condemnation of the devil. Moreover, he must have a good report of them which are without; lest he fall into reproach and the snare of the devil.

These are maturity qualifications dealing with personal conduct and character.

Christ has also authorized His people to teach and baptize in His name.

> All power is given unto me in heaven and in earth. Go ye therefore, and teach all nations, baptizing them in the name of the Father, and of the Son, and of the Holy Ghost: teaching them to observe all things whatsoever I have commanded you: and, lo, I am with you always, even unto the end of the world. Amen. (Matthew 28:18–20)

The command is not just to the early disciples; it is for all of the church age "even unto the end of the world." When a command is given, the authority to obey and fulfill that command is inherent in the command. It is ridiculous to think that Jesus, to whom all authority is given in heaven and earth, would command the church to go and teach all nations, baptize them in the name of the Father, Son, and Holy Ghost, and then say, "You don't have the authority to do what I commanded you to do."

Thus we learn from the scripture how God's authority is transmitted for service and leadership.

- The person must be saved from the wrath of God (i.e., he must have obtained mercy) by faith in Christ.
- He is given the necessary spiritual gifts as a sovereign act of the Holy Ghost at the time of salvation.
- He must have matured spiritually to the point that he meets the qualifications listed in the Bible.
- He must have developed his gifts to the point that he is competent to handle the task of overseeing and teaching God's people.
- He has been given the command of Christ to teach all nations and baptize in His name (Matthew 28:18–20).

After having reached that level of qualification, the candidate is ready to be ordained by a local church body that will recognize his qualifications, gifts, and maturity as evidence that he is in fact called of God. The laying on of hands may be employed in such ordination, but that does not give the individual anything God has not already given him.

Let's compare biblical ordination with ordination in the Mormon Church. In the Mormon Church, it is general practice to ordain most if not all twelve-year-old boys who are members to the office of deacon. Summarizing their responsibilities, they are charged with the responsibility to assist the teachers, warn, expound, exhort, teach, and invite all to come to Christ (*Doctrine and Covenants* Section 20:57–60).[4] They are to also watch over the church and to be standing ministers to the church (*Doctrine and Covenants* Section 84:111).[5] No consideration is given as to whether the twelve-year-old boys are mature enough to carry out the task, nor is any consideration given to whether they have received and developed the spiritual gifts of exhortation and teaching.

On the other hand, the Bible lists qualifications for deacons.

> Likewise, must the deacons be grave, not double tongued, not given to much wine, not greedy of filthy lucre; holding the mystery of the faith in a pure conscience. And let these also first be proved; then let them use the office of a deacon, being found blameless. Even so must their wives be grave, not slanderers, sober, faithful in all things. Let the deacons be husbands of one wife, ruling their children and their own houses well. For they that have used the office of a deacon well purchase to themselves a good degree, and great boldness in the faith which is in Christ Jesus. (1 Timothy 3:8–13)

In the Mormon Church, it is customary to ordain all fourteen-year-old boys to the office of teacher. Again summarizing, teachers are charged with the responsibility to

> watch over the church always, to be with and strengthen them; and to see that there is no iniquity in the church, neither hardness with each other, neither lying, backbiting nor evil speaking; and to see that the church

meet together often, and also see that all members do
their duty. (*Doctrine and Covenants* Section 20:53–59)[6]

No significant measures are taken to be sure all fourteen-year-old males
are gifted and mature and qualified enough to take on a task of such
magnitude. Do they all possess the maturity and courage necessary
to identify and rebuke iniquity, hardness, lying, backbiting, and evil-
speaking? Are they all qualified to identify and rebuke iniquity in the
adults of the church?

As a twelve-year-old deacon and a fourteen-year-old teacher in the
Mormon Church, I certainly had no such ability to "watch over the
church and strengthen it; to see that all members do their duty; to be
a standing minister in the church and warn and expound and teach."
Neither have I seen any twelve- or fourteen-year-olds capable of such
responsibility in any church. Even the Lord Jesus did not begin His
formal ministry until He was about thirty. I cannot believe the Lord
would in turn assign such heavy duties of the ministry to youth.

I conclude that Joseph Smith was in error concerning his doctrine of
the priesthood and its offices and in his doctrine concerning the laying
on of hands and transmission of authority. No, the church was not taken
from the earth after the apostles died. God has always had His faithful
ones; He has always delegated His authority to them, given them gifts,
and empowered them to do His bidding. It was no idle statement when
the Lord said, "I will build my church, and the gates of hell shall not
prevail against it" (Matthew 16:18).

CHAPTER 6

——————◇——————

THE ONLY TRUE GOD

Many times, I have been in testimony meetings in which I listened to person after person saying that he or she "knew" that Joseph Smith was a true prophet and that the Church of Jesus Christ of Latter-Day Saints was the true church. I wonder if those sincere people really testified to something they actually knew to be a fact or were merely stating what they sincerely believed.

Webster's New Collegiate Dictionary defines *testimony* as "firsthand authentication of a fact: EVIDENCE, A public profession of a religious experience." A personal testimony can be simply a statement of a belief without supporting evidence. However, if a testimony is meant to be a statement of truth, it must also be based on fact.

I am convinced that the testimony of most Mormon people is based primarily on some religious experience they had. It could be anything from being convinced that the Mormon Church is true because others they know and respect say it is true to having experienced burning feelings in their breasts. Perhaps they have experienced some kind of supernatural manifestation. Some say they have. It could be from God, or it could be from the enemy.

If the purpose of the manifestation is to lead a person away from the only true God or to lead a person to continue following a false god, the manifestation would have been from the enemy. Whatever the experience that led to the deep convictions, neither the experience nor the conviction changes the facts. "He that trusteth in his own heart is a fool: but whoso walketh wisely, he shall be delivered" (Proverbs 28:26).

Once, most of humankind believed the world was flat; people believed it sincerely and thought the idea of a spherical earth was ridiculous. But all the sincere belief in the world did not change the fact. Jesus said to the Father, "Thy word is truth" (John 17:17). No experience can ever supersede the authority of God's Word. Reliance on experience rather than on God's Word will be disastrous.

Joseph Smith's prophecies did not come true, and that is a fact. The serious and unsolvable problems in the reliability of the Book of Mormon are a fact. The Mormon teachings concerning priesthood, church offices, and the laying on of hands for the transmission of authority are not in accord with the Bible, and that is a fact. The Book of Mormon because of its unreliability and admission to internal error, the Doctrine and Covenants because of its false prophecies, The Pearl of Great Price because of its teaching of the multiplicity of gods in the creation account (and for many other reasons) simply do not measure up to the rigid standards that each book of the Bible had to pass to be recognized as the Word of God. And that is a fact.

People might testify that they know Joseph Smith was a true prophet and that the Mormon Church is the true church based on experience or feeling, but I will testify that I know Joseph Smith was not a true prophet and that the Mormon Church is not the true church, and I will base my testimony on fact. There was a time when I too would have testified in favor of Joseph Smith and the Mormon Church, but at that time, I did not know all the facts. Again, Proverbs 12:14 tells us, "There is a way that seemeth right unto a man but the end thereof are the ways of death." To escape the wrath of God, one's religious faith must more than just seem right or feel right; it must *be* right.

Has God provided a prophet to lead the church today? Since the beginning of the church age, Christ has been Prophet, Priest, and King to the church as well as being the Head of the church. The church (all those who believe in the only true God and trust in Christ as their Savior) is very different from the nation of Israel. The church has no geographical boundaries. The church is not made up of the Jewish people as was Israel; it is made up of Jew and Gentile alike (Ephesians 2:11–18). Christ is Head of the church (Colossians 1:18) and its chief

Shepherd, while the elders are the undershepherds who serve under the headship of Christ in the local church (1 Peter 5:1–4).

There is nothing in the Bible about a prophet who is to head up a church hierarchy to rule over all local churches. Nowhere in the New Testament do we find a first presidency consisting of a prophet and two counselors who head up the church and preside over the apostles. We do not need and should not have a prophet to oversee the church today other than the Lord Jesus Christ.

There should be continuing revelation from God to man according to the LDS church. At the return of Christ, there probably will be further revelation since He will be here in person. I do not believe there will be further revelation until that time. Revelation was the last book of the Bible written, and God instructed that there should be no more added to the book (Revelation 22:18–19). Twice in that chapter, Jesus said that he was coming quickly (vv. 7, 20). John was not to seal the prophecy because "the time is at hand" (v. 10). The return of Christ is the next major event to take place from heaven, and nothing is to be added to the revelation already given until that happens.

But let's assume that I'm wrong and that there is to be further revelation in written form. It is obvious that if it is from the only true God, it will be on the same level as the books of the Bible. The *Book of Mormon*, the *Doctrine and Covenants*, and *The Pearl of Great Price* all fall short of meeting the rigorous standards for recognizing the books of the Bible as God's Word, so they could not be God's revelation.

The serious problems in Mormon teaching and scripture I have shared with you in this book are only a tiny smattering of what has been discovered and written on the subject. I have no desire to simply duplicate the volumes that have already been written on the subject. What I have shared with you is meant to show you the great difference between the Mormon religion and true Christianity. I have striven to give you information you can quickly find to read for yourself to see if I have represented the facts correctly. I hope you will investigate for yourself.

I want to share with you something more about the wonderful God to whom I belong. God has been the almighty God from everlasting to everlasting and is also the Creator of all that was created. He created through His Son Jesus Christ, who existed eternally with the Father.

> In the beginning was the Word, and the Word was
> with God, and the Word was God. The same was in
> the beginning with God. All things were made by him;
> and without him was not anything made that was made.
> (John 1:1–3; Revelation 19:7–13 identifies the Word as
> Jesus Christ)

God's creation is simply beyond description. In our world of jet travel, we sometimes forget how immense the earth is and how full it is of intricately created life. It all testifies to the infinite knowledge and power of the Creator. The apostle Paul told us that there were three things we could know about the Creator just by observing His creation. First, He is the Creator. Second, we can know His eternal power. Third, we can know His Godhead, i.e., that He is God and in headship over all "for the invisible things of him from the creation of the world are clearly seen, being understood by the things that are made, even his eternal power and Godhead; so that they are without excuse" (Romans 1:20).

There is simply no excuse to not know this according to the Bible (Romans 1:20). One need only observe creation to know that God is and to know how great He is. He made the stars (Genesis 1:16) and knows the names of every star: "He telleth the number of the stars; he calleth them all by *their* names" (Psalm 147:4).

Isaiah declared God's greatness to Israel.

> Who hath measured the waters in the hollow of his
> hand, and meted out heaven with the span (of his hand),
> and comprehended the dust of the earth in a measure,
> and weighed the mountains in scales, and the hills in
> a balance? Who hath directed the Spirit of the LORD,
> or being his counselor hath taught him? With whom
> took he counsel, and who instructed him, and taught
> him the path of judgment, and taught him knowledge,
> and shewed to him the way of understanding? (Isaiah
> 40:12–14)

The obvious answer is that no one but God could possibly do these things.

> Behold, the nations are as a drop of a bucket, and are counted as the small dust of a balance: behold, he taketh up the isles as a very little thing. And Lebanon is not sufficient to burn, nor the beasts thereof sufficient for a burnt offering. All the nations before him are as nothing; and they are counted to him as less than nothing, and vanity. (Isaiah 40:15–17)

With all the awesome power of the armies, navies, and the nuclear arsenals of the world, God still says the nations are to Him less than nothing. Through these words, God was trying to snap people out of their stupefying idol worship and get them to see Him.

> To whom then will ye liken God? Or what likeness will ye compare unto him? Have ye not known? Have ye not heard? Hath it not been told you from the beginning? Have ye not understood from the foundations of the earth? It is he that sitteth upon the circle of the earth, and the inhabitants thereof are as grasshoppers; that stretch out the heavens as a curtain, and spreadeth them out as a tent to dwell in: That bringeth the princes to nothing; he maketh the judges of the earth as vanity. (Isaiah 40:18, 21–23)

Where is Alexander the Great, Stalin, or Hitler? God brings the princes of the earth to nothing.

As great as the earth and all that is in it is, nothing gives us a glimpse of the greatness of God as do the starry heavens. More than once I have heard even Mormon people say that God is the Almighty and could not be an exalted man. They based their conclusion on nothing but the time they spent gazing at the stars and being struck with the awesome immensity of it all.

> To whom then will ye liken me, or shall I be equal saith
> the Holy One. Lift up your eyes on high, and behold
> who hath created these things, that bringeth out their
> host (stars) by number: he calleth them all by names by
> the greatness of his might, for that he is strong in power;
> not one faileth. (Isaiah 40:25–26)

It was once thought that there were no more stars than could be seen with the naked eye. With the advent of modern telescopes, it has been discovered that the universe is unfathomable in size and is continually expanding. The galaxies appear to be traveling away from each other at fantastic speeds. In Genesis 1:8, God called the firmament heaven. The Hebrew word for firmament is *raqia* (raw-kee-ah). The root meaning of the word had to do with metal plates being continually expanded by hammering. The idea as applied to the heavens is that of continuous expansion.[1] God revealed the truth about the expanding universe long before science discovered it.

The distances within the expanding universe are so immense that they must be measured in light-years (the distance light travels in one year, about six trillion miles). The distance from the earth to the sun is about 93 million miles. If we were to travel the distance of only one light-year, we would travel the equivalent of 33,000 times to the sun and back. The Milky Way galaxy, in which our sun and solar system reside, is 10,000 light-years thick at the center and 100,000 light-years across. It contains some 100,000,000,000 stars averaging in size about like our sun. And there are estimated to be billions of galaxies in the universe averaging the size of the Milky Way. Jeremiah and the writer of Hebrews said that the stars were as innumerable as the sands of the sea (Hebrews 11:12; Jeremiah 33:22). As far back as 1963, radio telescopes discovered quasars at the outer edge of the known universe, and they shine with the intensity of a trillion suns.

What is it all for? Psalm 19:1–2 explains it: "The heavens declare the glory of God; and the firmament sheweth his handywork. Day unto day uttereth speech, and night unto night sheweth knowledge." Try to comprehend the magnitude of it all. Of course our limited human minds cannot grasp it, but notice what Isaiah says in 40:26: "Lift up your eyes on high, and behold who hath created these things, that bringeth out their hosts by number: he calleth them all by names by the greatness of his might, for that he is strong in power; not one faileth." Can you get a glimpse of the majesty, glory, power, immensity and knowledge of God? His glory? God, the Creator of the universe and all things in it, knows the names of every star and every human being. "He telleth the number of the stars; he calleth them all by their names. Great is our LORD, and of great power; His understanding is infinite" (Psalm 147:4–5). "O Lord, thou hast searched me, and known me. Thou knowest my downsitting and mine uprising, thou understandeth my thought afar off. Thou compassest my path and my lying down, and art acquainted with all my ways" (Psalm 139:1–2). He knows every hair on every human head (Matthew 10:30; Luke 12:7).

I feel compelled to answer a question many Mormon people have—how can God fill the universe and still be small enough to dwell in our hearts? By way of illustration, consider the atmosphere, which is large enough to cover the earth thirty to forty miles deep but small enough to enter our lungs. Why then does it seem impossible for the infinite God to fill the universe and dwell in the human heart? Scripture tells us a wonderful secret—God Himself lives in true believers.

> One God and Father of all, who is above all, and through all, *and in you all.* (Ephesians 4:6, emphasis added)

> To whom God would make known what is the riches of the glory of this mystery among the Gentiles; *which is Christ in you,* the hope of glory. (Colossians 1:27, emphasis added)

> What? Know ye not that your body is the temple of *the Holy Ghost which is in you,* which ye have of God, and ye are not your own? (1 Corinthians 6:19, emphasis added)

> Do not I fill heaven and earth? Saith the LORD. (Jeremiah 23:24)

God fills heaven and earth, and He lives in believers in the persons of the Father, Son, and Holy Ghost. Those who scoff at revealed truth simply have not believed what God has stated about Himself.

Many Mormon people feel they cannot relate to a God of Spirit and insist that God must have a body of flesh and bone. This greatly limits our understanding of God and causes us to think of God as confined by time and space. Jesus told us plainly, "God is Spirit and those who worship Him must worship Him in spirit and in truth" (John 4:24).

But God certainly does understand our need to have something in Him to which we can better relate. To meet this need, He gave us Jesus Christ, who was born on earth a human and has a glorified and resurrected body of flesh and bone. He lived as a Man on earth and suffered pain, hardship, temptation, grief, and sorrow. Certainly we can relate to that. God meets our every need. The Father is Spirit while the Son is both Spirit and body to whom we can more readily relate.

While pondering the majesty of God, David declared, "What is man that thou art mindful of him?" (Psalm 8:4) That is truly a humble cry from a man who recognized his insignificance in light of God's greatness. The very epitome of pride, on the other hand, is seen in Lucifer when he boastfully declared, "I will be like the Most High" (the full quote is in Isaiah 14:13–15).

> For thou hast said in thine heart, I will ascend into heaven, I will exalt my throne above the stars of God: I will sit also in the mount of the congregation, in the sides of the north: I will ascend above the heights of the clouds; I will be like the Most High. Yet thou shalt be brought down to hell, to the sides of the pit.

Is your goal to be like the Most High? Do you believe your priesthood can make a human being that averages six feet tall and has approximately a three-pound brain into an almighty, omnipresent, omniscient creator who can fill the universe and create billions of galaxies by his spoken word? If you seriously believe that, you will suffer the same fate as Satan. Do not dare look into the heavens and boast, "I will become like God." Lucifer did, and look what happened to him. Neither can I believe in a mere exalted man who is thought to have organized one or perhaps a few planets over which he reigns.

The almighty, eternal, and unchanging God created the universe and everything in it including the enormously complex DNA molecule packed with genetic information that replicates itself and enables every living thing to replicate itself after its own kind. This almighty God said, "I am he, before me there was no God formed, neither shall there be after me. I, even I am the LORD; and beside me there is no savior" (Isaiah 43:1–11). Do you believe Him?

If a mere exalted man is God, serve him. But if the almighty Creator of the heavens and the earth is God, serve Him. Choose this day whom you will serve. I have chosen to serve the almighty, unchanging, everlasting Creator of all things. I have chosen to believe Him; He says there are no other gods. I have chosen to trust His Son Jesus Christ for salvation from my sins. I have chosen to serve in the one true church, the body and bride of Christ, which consists of all who serve the only true God and have trusted in His Son Jesus Christ as Savior and Lord.

My priesthood in Christ gives me authority to enter the presence of God at any time and without fear (Hebrews 4:16). The command of Christ and the gifts of the Holy Ghost given to me give me God's authority to preach the gospel of Christ to everyone everywhere, to baptize in His name, and to teach and lead in the local church. And yes, there is more—much more. By the God of all creation, all spiritual blessings in heavenly places have been given to me in Christ (Ephesians 1–3).

The true exaltation that God has planned for His beloved creature, man, is the gift of His righteousness and elevation to the position of sonship with all spiritual blessings in Christ (Ephesians 1:1–12). It comes not by striving for one's own righteousness as did the Jews.

> Brethren, my heart's desire and prayer to God for Israel is that they might be saved. For I bear them record that they have a zeal for God, but not according to knowledge. For they being ignorant of God's righteousness, and going about to establish their own righteousness, have not submitted themselves unto the righteousness of

God. For Christ is the end of the law for righteousness
to everyone that believeth. (Romans 10:1–4)

Righteousness, right standing before God, comes not by striving for
godhood that never has been promised by the true God. True exaltation
comes through true humility: "Humble yourselves therefore under the
mighty hand of God, that he may exalt you in due time" (1 Peter 5:6).
It comes through simple confession of one's unworthiness.

> If we say that we have no sin, we deceive ourselves, and
> the truth is not in us. If we confess our sins, he is faithful
> and just to forgive us our sins, and to cleanse us from
> all unrighteousness. If we say that we have not sinned,
> we make him a liar, and his word is not in us. (1 John
> 1:8–10)

The gift of righteousness comes by believing in the heart, confessing
with the mouth, and calling on the Lord for forgiveness and eternal life.

First, last, and always, God is concerned with the human heart. "The
heart is deceitful above all things, and desperately wicked" (Jeremiah
17:9). This does not mean that every person is as wicked as can be all
the time. It does not mean that man is incapable of doing good before
being saved. It means every part of the human individual is affected
by sin—mind, emotions, will, and body. It means every person has a
fallen human nature. We need do nothing but observe the behavior of
children to realize that deep within their nature is sinful selfishness.
They are not taught to be selfish; it is part of their nature. The apostle
Paul saw this in himself and wrote, "For I know that in me (that is, in
my flesh), dwelleth no good thing" (Romans 7:18). In verses 15–25, he
described his desperate but futile attempt to overcome the power of
sin in his life. His nature was corrupt, and he found help only in Jesus
Christ. An organized church cannot redeem humans; an organized
church cannot change the human heart; the heart can be changed only
by the power of God working in it.

We must believe in our hearts to be accepted by God.

That if thou shalt confess with thy mouth the Lord
Jesus, and believe in thine heart that God hath raised
him from the dead, thou shalt be saved. For with the
heart man believeth unto righteousness; and with
the mouth confession is made unto salvation. For the
Scripture saith, whosoever believeth on him shall not
be ashamed. For there is no difference between the Jew
and the Greek: for the same Lord over all is rich unto
all that call upon him. For whosoever shall call upon
the name of the Lord shall be saved. (Romans 10:9–10)

God's love is as infinite as is His power. He reaches out to all in loving-
kindness. Right in the depths of Israel's idolatry, God continued to
strengthen and bless them for a time. They worshipped their idols, and
when they saw the answer to prayer, they thought their little gods had
answered. In Isaiah 45:5, the Lord said to them, "I girded thee, though
thou hast not known me."

Perhaps when you prayed, you believed an exalted man was
answering your prayers. Your prayers were answered by the only true
God, who loves you even though you might not have known Him. He
has been caring for you all along, and perhaps, He is revealing Himself
to you for the first time through the scripture shared in this book. Will
you not come to the true God and seek His forgiveness by faith in
Christ? The Lord Jesus Christ loves you and invites you: "Come unto
me, all ye that labour and are heavy laden, and I will give you rest"
(Matthew 11:29).

For God so loved the world, that he gave his only
begotten Son, that whosoever believeth in him should
not perish, but have everlasting life. For God sent not
his Son into the world to condemn the world; but that
the world through him might be saved. *He that believeth
on him is not condemned: but he that believeth not is
condemned already,* because he hath not believed in
the name of the only begotten Son of God. And this
is the condemnation, that light is come into the world,

and men loved darkness rather than light, because their deeds were evil. For everyone that doeth evil hateth the light because their deeds were evil. For everyone that doeth evil hateth the light, neither cometh to the light, that his deeds should be reproved. But he that doeth truth cometh to the light, that his deeds may be made manifest, that they are wrought in God. (John 3:16–21, emphasis added)

I am the way, the truth and the life: no man cometh unto the Father, but by me. (John 14:6)

James 2:20–26 may have been bothering you with regard to faith: "But wilt thou know, O vain man, that faith without works is dead? … For as the body without the spirit is dead, so faith without works is dead also." James is clarifying the kind or the quality of faith needed to result in eternal life. It is simply an obedient faith. It is more than an intellectual acknowledgement of Christ. For example, if you believe that theft is wrong but you steal anyway, your faith is dead. If you believe that you are to speak the truth but you don't, your faith is dead. If you believe that you need to confess your sins and receive Christ as your Savior but don't, your faith is dead. Good works, which are subsequent to God's forgiveness, demonstrate an obedient, genuine faith, but good works do not purchase or earn forgiveness. Forgiveness is the gift of God through genuine obedient faith (Ephesians 2:4–10).

A FINAL WORD ABOUT SALVATION FROM SIN

In my over three decades of ministry, I have discovered that most people are trying to get to heaven by their good works as if their good deeds could somehow pay for their sin and purchase a pass into heaven. We could liken this to marathon runners who join the race somewhere, perhaps even inches, after the starting line. They may run hard, skillfully, and even sacrificially. They may even cross the finish line first, but they are immediately disqualified because they did not start at the starting line. Remember, Jesus told of such people when He said,

> Not everyone that saith unto me, Lord, Lord, shall enter
> into the kingdom of heaven; but he that doeth the will
> of my Father which is in heaven. Many will say to me
> in that day, Lord, Lord, have we not prophesied in thy
> name? and in thy name have cast out devils? and in
> thy name done many wonderful works? And then will
> I profess unto them, I never knew you: depart from me,
> ye that work iniquity. (Matthew 7:21–23)

Would not those be horrible words to hear when you stand before the Lord Jesus Christ in judgment hoping to get into heaven? Can you imagine a whole lifetime of good works, even miraculous works, counted by the Savior as "works of iniquity"? Doing the will of the Father is first and above all else trusting in the Savior He provided for the forgiveness of sin; otherwise, we remain under God's condemnation, "condemned already" (John 3:18).

If you believe in the only true God of the Bible and in His Son Jesus Christ, who died on the cross to pay for your sins and rose from the dead, here is the starting line. Ask the Lord Jesus Christ to forgive all your sins, the ones you remember and the ones you don't remember. Trust Him to do so. Then follow Him and live for Him as your personal Savior.

Jesus said that those who believe in him have everlasting life! He was speaking in the present tense. One who truly trusts in the Lord Jesus for forgiveness of sin is not condemned and has passed from death into life. Jesus has not lied to us. You can trust Him to forgive your sins, which puts you across the starting line into eternal life.

> He that believeth on the Son hath everlasting life: and
> he that believeth not the Son shall not see life; but the
> wrath of God abideth on him. (John 3:36)

> Verily, verily, I say unto you, He that heareth my word,
> and believeth on him that sent me, hath everlasting life,
> and shall not come into condemnation; but is passed
> from death unto life. (John 5:24)

> Verily, verily, I say unto you, He that believeth on me
> hath everlasting life. (John 6:47)

You may wonder about repentance. Turning away from belief in a false god and a false religious system is repentance. You may be aware of other sins as well. Turn from your sins. Confess all your sins, and ask the Lord to forgive you.

A SUGGESTED PRAYER IF THIS IS WHAT YOU REALLY BELIEVE

Dear God, I believe that You are the Creator of the entire universe and that there are no other gods beside You. I believe that Jesus Christ is Your Son. I believe He died on the cross to pay for my sins and rose from the dead. I trust Jesus Christ as my Savior. I ask You to forgive all my sins, the ones I remember and the ones I don't remember. Thank You for forgiving me and giving me eternal life. In Jesus's name, amen.

CHAPTER 7

—◇—

LIVING ETERNAL LIFE

The Lord Jesus Christ made it clear that when we trust in Him for forgiveness of sin, we have passed from the condition of spiritual death (which Adam brought into the world, Romans 5:12) into the condition of spiritual life (which Jesus Christ brought into the world, John 5:24).

How are we then to live this new life? First, we need to understand what the Lord's purpose is for us. God created us in His image and likeness (Genesis 1:26–27). Four times in those two verses, it is stated that God created man in His image and likeness. It must be very important to be stated four times.

Mormonism insists that the image of God means God has a physical body, but that completely misses the point. God is a Spirit; Jesus told us that plainly in John 4:23–24. Jesus, who created all things (John 1:1–3, 14) did not have a body until the virgin birth. The Holy Ghost does not have a body. God's image and likeness spoken of in Genesis 1:26–27 mean God's moral image. God's moral attributes are as follows: He is holy (Leviticus 11:44–45), righteous (Psalm 89:14), just (Psalm 89:14), truth (Psalm 89:14), love (1 John 4:16), good (Exodus 34:6), mercy (Psalm 89:14), gracious (Titus 2:11), and benevolent (Matthew 5:45). The moral attributes of the Lord Jesus Christ are the same—He is holy (Acts 3:14), righteous (1 John 2:1), just (Acts 3:14), truth (John 14:6), merciful (Luke 7:48–50), good, (Matthew 19:14), love (Ephesians 3:19), gracious (John 1:14), and benevolent (Philippians 4:19). His attributes are either stated or demonstrated.

So how do we know God created those moral attributes in Adam and Eve? We know it because the purpose of the Lord Jesus Christ is to redeem us and restore us to His image (Romans 8:29). His image does not mean eyes, ears, mouth, hands, feet, and so on. Why would He conform and restore us to something we already have? His image refers to His moral nature, or as Peter called it, His divine nature (2 Peter 1:4). That moral image was severely damaged (irreparably damaged without God's intervention through Christ) in the first act of sinful disobedience Adam and Eve committed (Genesis 3).

The chart below illustrates what happened to Adam and Eve and all humankind as a result of their chosen disobedience and fall into sin.[1]

God's Moral Attributes in Man	Example of God's Divine Attributes Severely Damaged in Humanity by Adam and Eve's Fall into Sin; Humankind Acquired a Sin Nature
Holy, Leviticus 11:44–45	Separated from God, spiritually blind, profane, false worshipper, disobedient
Righteous, Psalm 89:14	Capable of thinking, desiring, and doing wrong; sinful attitudes and actions; haughty, hypocritical
Just, Psalm 89:14	Unjust, unfair, lacks a sense of right and wrong, pursues wrong
Truth, Psalm 89:14	Self-deceiving, covenant breaker, liar, cheat, suppresses the truth, actively promotes falsehoods
Love, 1 John 4:16	Unloving, uncaring, hateful, lustful, fornicator, adulterous, murderous
Good, Exodus 34:6	Despisers of what is good, lovers of pleasure, dishonor parents, envious, jealous
Mercy, Psalm 89:14	Unforgiving, grudge carrier, condemning, critical spirit
Gracious, Titus 2:11	Ill-mannered, crass, unkind, insensitive to others, uncontrolled anger, unthankful
Benevolent, Matthew 5:45	Selfish, stingy, unwilling to share, thieving

God's perfect and glorious moral attributes are shattered in us. We can do what is right but only to a degree. We can love but only imperfectly. We are incapable of God's perfection, and we are unable to get rid of the sin nature that is a part of us. Most of us do not choose to be as bad as we could be, but sin functions in us nonetheless.

Sin has a tremendous impact on our thinking, motivations, attitudes, self-evaluation, view of others, and behavior. Even a child does not have to be taught to lie or be selfish or unkind; that comes naturally from the fallen sin nature everyone inherits.

Our bodies are also affected by sin; we age, suffer, die, and return to the dust of the ground as God said to Adam. We have all inherited those sinful deficiencies and fall short of the glory of God. The apostle Paul explained it this way in Romans 5:12: "Wherefore, just as by one man (Adam) sin entered into the world and death by sin; and so death passed upon all men, for that all have sinned."

Even after salvation by faith in Christ, we still have the sin nature to deal with. This causes a great conflict in us as the apostle Paul explained in Romans 7:14–25. What a tremendous struggle occurs in the heart of redeemed people. Paul wanted to obey God, but instead, he often committed the very sin he hated: "For that which I do I allow not: for what I would, that do I not; but what I hate, that I do" (Romans 7:15).

He acknowledged that the law of God was good: "If then I do that which I would not, I consent unto the law that it is good" (v. 16). Then Paul identified the problem—indwelling sin: "Now then it is no more I that do it, but sin that dwelleth in me" (v. 17).

If you have repented and received and trusted in the Lord Jesus Christ as your Savior, the real you is now the divine nature God gave you. However, you still have indwelling sin to deal with. What a tremendous struggle Paul found it to be to try to get free of the problem of indwelling sin: "O wretched man that I am! Who shall deliver me from the body of this death?"(v. 24) He gave the answer in verse 25: "I thank God through Jesus Christ our Lord." Jesus Christ is the Who, but the how Paul did not answer until chapter 12.

However, there is something else we need to understand first—it is God's purpose to change us until we are conformed to the very spiritual image of the Lord Jesus Christ: "And we know that all things work together for good to them that love God, to them who are called according to his purpose" (Romans 8:28). Verse 29 tells us that purpose: "For whom He did foreknow, He also did predestinate to be conformed to the image of His Son, that He might be the firstborn among many brethren." We are Jesus's brothers not by birth but by adoption (Ephesians 1:4–5).

God uses everything that happens to the believer in Christ, both the good and the bad, to gradually conform the believer to the image of Christ. We are to glorify God; we are to put God's divine nature on display before the world by the attitudes we display, the lives we live, the words we say, and even by our thoughts and motivations.

We can accomplish that by renewing our minds.

> I beseech you therefore, brethren, by the mercies of God, that ye present your bodies a living sacrifice, holy, acceptable unto God, which is your reasonable service. And be not conformed to this world: *but be ye transformed by the renewing of your mind* that ye may prove what is that good, and acceptable, and perfect will of God. (Romans 12:1–2, emphasis added)

God uses the indwelling Christ, the Word of God, and circumstances in life good and bad to change us from the inside out by renewing our minds. This is not just trying to act like good people on the outside (what people can observe); it is a supernatural change from the inside. Read the rest of the book of Romans to get the details. This in brief is how we are to live the Christian life. But what will the eternal future be like for the lost and the redeemed?

THE FUTURE OF THE UNSAVED

We have mentioned this before, but it bears repeating. We need to consider what the eternal future holds for people who have not believed in the only begotten Son of God for the forgiveness of sin. They remain eternally guilty, unclean, and contaminated by sin. Even punishment in hell does not cleanse a person of sin. The blood of Christ is God's only provision for sin. Therefore, their punishment is eternal.

Jesus Christ is the only way back to the Father. Reject Him or neglect Him and you will have no recourse. In Luke 16:19–31, Jesus warned us of the consequences of not taking Him seriously. This is the story Jesus told of the rich man and Lazarus after they died. Being rich or poor is not the plan of salvation. But in this case, the rich man was the one who did not love and follow the Lord. His torment in fire is unmistakable.

The clearest statement on the destiny of the unsaved is in Revelation 20:11–15, the great white throne judgment just before the new heaven and the new earth are revealed.

> And I saw a great white throne, and him that sat on it, from whose face the earth and the heaven fled away; and there was found no place for them. And I saw the dead, small and great, stand before God; and the books were opened: and another book was opened, which is *the book* of life: and the dead were judged out of those things which were written in the books, according to their works. And the sea gave up the dead which were in it; and death and hell delivered up the dead which were in them: and they were judged every man according to their works. And death and hell were cast into the lake of fire. This is the second death. And whosoever was not found written in the book of life was cast into the lake of fire.

This is not enjoyable to communicate, but it is the Word of God, and it is the truth. It is very important to remember the lost condition of humankind and from what the Lord has saved us. It is also important to remember that others are in desperate need of salvation. Jesus told us that those who did not believe in Him, the true Christ, were condemned already (John 3:16–17). Everyone needs the Savior.

THE FUTURE OF THE REDEEMED

Those who have come to a saving faith in the Lord Jesus Christ are not condemned and will never face the judgment of condemnation. We who are saved from the wrath of God will however be judged for our service for Christ and given various rewards. This judgment is called the judgment seat of Christ and is told of in 1 Corinthians 3:11–15.

> For other foundation can no man lay than that is laid, which is Jesus Christ. Now if any man build upon this foundation gold, silver, precious stones, wood, hay, stubble; every man's work shall be made manifest: for the day shall declare it, because it shall be revealed by fire; and the fire shall try every man's work of what sort it is. If any man's work abide which he hath built thereupon, he shall receive a reward. If any man's work shall be burned, he shall suffer loss: but he himself shall be saved; yet so as by fire.

The gold, silver, and precious stones represent those things we do, say, and think that are of eternal value, namely, our service to Christ. The wood, hay, and stubble represent things we do, say, and think that are of no eternal value, and they are burned. There is no reward for those things.

What are the rewards? Many of them are special honors given by the Lord Jesus. They are the crown of life (James 1:12), the crown of righteousness (2 Timothy 4:7–10), the crown incorruptible (1 Corinthians 9:24–25), and the crown of glory that does not fade away for faithful elders (1 Peter 5:4). See those passages below.

> I have fought a good fight, I have finished *my* course, I have kept the faith: Henceforth there is laid up for me a crown of righteousness, which the Lord, the righteous judge, shall give me at that day: and not to me only, but unto all them also that love his appearing. (2 Timothy 4:7–8)

> Know ye not that they which run in a race run all, but one receiveth the prize? So run, that ye may obtain. And every man that striveth for the mastery is temperate in all things. Now they do it to obtain a corruptible

crown; but we an incorruptible. I therefore so run, not as uncertainly; so fight I, not as one that beateth the air: But I keep under my body, and bring it into subjection: lest that by any means, when I have preached to others, I myself should be a castaway. (1 Corinthians 9:24–27)

The elders which are among you I exhort, who am also an elder, and a witness of the sufferings of Christ, and also a partaker of the glory that shall be revealed: Feed the flock of God which is among you, taking the oversight thereof, not by constraint, but willingly; not for filthy lucre, but of a ready mind; Neither as being lords over God's heritage, but being ensamples to the flock. And when the chief Shepherd shall appear, ye shall receive a crown of glory that fadeth not away. (1 Peter 5:1–4)

Blessed *is* the man that endureth temptation: for when he is tried, he shall receive the crown of life, which the Lord hath promised to them that love him. (James 1:12)

Also, there is assurance of rewards in other passages. Jesus assured us that even a simple act of kindness such as giving a child a cup of cold water would result in a reward.

And whosoever shall give to drink unto one of these little ones a cup of cold water only in the name of a disciple, verily I say unto you, he shall in no wise lose his reward. (Matthew 10:42)

Jesus spoke a parable in Luke 19:11–27 showing that those who were faithful to use what He had given would receive great reward. One of my favorite passages on rewards is a simple statement in Hebrews 6:10: "For God is not unrighteous to forget your work and labour of love, which ye have shewed toward his name, in that ye have ministered to the saints, and do minister."

Here, I think it is important to clarify again the difference between salvation from sin and reward for service. We are so prone to think in terms of earning our way to salvation that we easily slip into the old mind-set of earning our way to heaven. Salvation is always spoken of as a gift, for example, in John 4:10, Romans 6:23, Ephesians 2:8–9, and Titus 3:5. Rewards are given for good works as noted in the passages printed in the paragraphs above. Also, salvation is a present possession for the believer in Christ—John 3:36 and John 5:24, 6:47. Rewards are future—to be awarded at the judgment seat of Christ (1 Corinthians 3:9–15).

WHERE WILL WE LIVE?

After the judgment seat of Christ, believers will return with Christ to rule and reign with Him on earth for a thousand years (Revelation 19:1–20:6). We will reign over those who live through the great tribulation judgments on earth and their offspring. Jesus told of them in Matthew 25:31–34. Jesus was answering the disciples' questions about His coming and the end of the world (see Matthew 24:3). We are told in Colossians 3:1–4 that when He appears, we will appear with him in glory. And in Revelation 19, the Lamb's wife is identified and granted white linen, which represents the righteousness of the saints (those who have trusted in Christ as their personal Savior). Those who are dressed in white linen will return with Christ (Revelation 19:7–14).

After the millennial reign, we will live with Christ on the new heaven and the new earth (Revelation 21:1–7). The New Jerusalem, which will come down from heaven onto the new earth is described in Revelation 21:9–27. Twelve thousand furlongs equals 1,400 to 1,500 miles long, wide, and high. The city is immense and would cover nearly all the Western United States. The nations on earth and the kings of the nations will enter it and bring the glory of the nations before God in worship. We will be free to do everything our hearts, minds, and gifts enable us to do because there will be no sin in us. We will have no desire to even think of anything sinful. Everything we do will be right in the sight of God. We will not be gods, nor will we even aspire to be. It was never God's intention that we be gods but that we be perfectly righteous humans with resurrected, glorified spiritual bodies that will live forever (1 Corinthians 15). There will be no tears, death, sorrow, crying, or pain because former things will have passed away (Revelation 21:4).

Jesus knows us perfectly—our likes and dislikes. He has gone to prepare a place for us, and when we see it, it will be glorious beyond what we can imagine, and yet it will feel like home.

> Let not your heart be troubled: ye believe in God, believe also in me. In my Father's house are many mansions: if *it were* not *so*, I would have told you. I go to prepare a place for you. And if I go and prepare a place for you, I will come again, and receive you unto myself; that where I am, *there* ye may be also. (John 14:1–3)

WILL WE BE MARRIED?

The Sadducees who did not believe in resurrection tried to stump Jesus by asking him what they thought was an impossible question to answer (Matthew 22:23–32). They asked Him if a woman married and her husband died, then she married his brother and he died, and this continued until she had married seven brothers, whose wife she would be in the resurrection. Jesus answered, "Ye do err, not knowing the scriptures, nor the power of God. For in the resurrection they neither marry, nor are given in marriage, but are as the angels of God in heaven."

Human marriage is not eternal. Bearing billions of spirit children to populate planets will not be your destiny. Human marriage is a symbol of the great eternal marriage between Christ and His body of true believers, the church. The marriage supper of the Lamb fulfills the symbolism of human marriage (Revelation 19:5–9). Our family members who have trusted in Christ for themselves will be there. And we can freely associate with them all we wish, but there will not be marriage in the eternal future. Do you believe Jesus when He said there will be no marriage in the resurrection? What He has for us is far better than human marriage.

> And he that sat upon the throne said, Behold, I make all things new. And he said unto me, Write: for these words

are true and faithful. And he said unto me, it is done. I am Alpha and Omega, the beginning and the end. I will give unto him that is athirst of the fountain of the water of life freely. He that overcometh shall inherit all things; and I will be his God, and he shall be My son. (Revelation 21:5–7)

Only the living creator God of the Bible is God. There are none before Him, and there will be none after Him. God is

- omniscient (Proverbs 15:3; Psalm 147:5; Hebrews 4:13; Matthew 10:30),
- omnipotent (Genesis 17:1; Jeremiah 32:17; Revelation 19:6),
- omnipresent (Jeremiah 23:23–24; Psalm 139:7–12; Acts 17:27–28),
- immutable (James 1:7; Malachi 3:6; Psalm 33:11), and
- sovereign (Matthew 20:15; Romans 9:20–21; 1 Chronicles 29:11; Ephesians 1:11).

No one else will be what God is in His attributes of omniscience, omnipotence, omnipresence, and immutability including His right to rule the universe. He alone is God. But you and I can become what He is in His moral attributes of holiness, righteousness, being just, truthful, loving, good, merciful, gracious, and benevolent. He loves you with all His heart. He designed you special and created you for Himself. He wants to redeem you and help you walk with Him. He actually wants you to glorify Him by your life, that is, He has chosen you to put Him on display before the world by the way you live and by what you say and believe, by your attitudes and actions, by becoming in your heart the very moral attributes mentioned above.

Will you love Him, worship Him, and serve Him? He has a wonderful eternal future ahead for you. Will you surrender? Will you trust Him?

I thank you for this opportunity to explain. If you are a member of the Church of Jesus Christ of Latter-Day Saints, reading this may not have been easy for you, and I sincerely appreciate the time, thought, prayer, and perhaps the emotions you have invested as you read this book. Thank you for taking the time to consider what I have said. The Mormon pioneer spirit is my heritage, but the Mormon faith is no longer my faith. My prayer for you is that God will lead you to eternal life: "And this is life eternal, that they might know thee, the only true God, and Jesus Christ, whom thou hast sent" (John 17:3).

APPENDIX

FINDING A GOOD CHURCH

You may be facing a daunting task as you look for another church. You may feel very alone not knowing how to begin. Some people who leave the LDS church just give up on church altogether. Feelings of fear over what church leaders, friends, and family might think or say may discourage you. You may be facing real persecution. It is very important, however, to find a loving church where you can be spiritually nourished.

Each local church is made up of people with different personalities, and together, they give each church its unique personality. When I first started attending a local Baptist church, everything seemed strange except for a few people I knew. I do not recall having attended any church outside the LDS church prior to that. Don't worry; you will get through it. If you have trusted the Lord Jesus Christ as your very own Savior, He has an adventurous life ahead for you. Everything you encounter both good and bad He will faithfully use to help you grow in the grace and in the knowledge of the Lord Jesus Christ (Romans 8:28–38). Look forward to the adventure. Pray and trust Him every step of the way.

Here are a few guidelines. Look for a church that has its doctrine correct. You may not feel you know enough, but you already know what you have learned in this book. Ask for a doctrinal statement from the church and study it (Titus 2:1). It should have scriptural references supporting each subject. Ask the pastor or pastoral staff to explain what you do not understand.

Look for a church where the people reach out to you and want to include you. It is important that the people you fellowship with are mature enough to love you and that you learn to love with God's love also (John 13:34–35).

Look for a church that has opportunities for service. Usually, there is something you can help with that is simple but important. Ask the pastor (Psalm 100:2; Ephesians 2:10).

Look for a church that has an evangelism emphasis of some type. The church needs to be reaching out to people to win them to Christ (Matthew 28:18–20).

Look for a church that practices baptism for those who have believed in Christ and know they are saved (Romans 6:1–4).

Look for a church that observes the Lord's Supper periodically. The bread and the cup are elements that help us remember the Lord's death, burial, and resurrection (1 Corinthians 11:23–26).

Look for a church where the leaders are spiritually mature and have a servant attitude (1 Peter 5:1–4; 1 Timothy 3:1–13).

Keep in mind that in every church, there are usually true believers and those who do not yet believe. There are those who are more mature in the faith and some less mature. People are learning and struggling to grow in Christ just as we are. Pray and trust God to lead you to the best church available (1 Peter 5:5–11).

NOTES

Later editions of the *Book of Mormon, Doctrine and Covenants*, and *The Pearl of Great Price* reflect the same wording and changes in wording noted in the older editions I have used.

I have not relied heavily on the work of the late Jerald Tanner and his wife, Sandra, in this book, but I have found what I have read of their works to be exhaustive, accurate, and factual.

PREFACE

1. A stake is a higher level of ecclesiastical organization within the Mormon church structure that gives oversight to several local churches in a specific geographical area. Each local church is called a ward. The stake presidency consists of the stake president and two counselors.

CHAPTER 1

1. For a detailed explanation of these doctrines as held by the Church of Jesus Christ of Latter-Day Saints, see *Mormon Doctrine* by Bruce R. McConkie, 238, 321, 557, 576–77, and the *Doctrine and Covenants* Sections 132:17–20, 37; 76:50–58; and 121:32.

CHAPTER 2

1. Josh McDowell, *Evidence that Demands a Verdict*, vol. 1 (San Bernardino, CA: Thomas Nelson, 1979), 39.

2. Ibid., 52.

3. Ibid., 50.

4. Ibid., 29.

5. For information supporting the claim that the *Book of Mormon* was translated by the gift and power of God, see *Book of Mormon* title page paragraph 1; *Book of Mormon*, Testimony of the Three Witnesses; *Book of Mormon*, Mormon 9:32–34; *Pearl of Great Price*, Joseph Smith 2:62, *Doctrine and Covenants* Section 17:1; *Book of Mormon*, Alma 37:23. Gazelem is identified as Joseph Smith Jun. [sic] in the *Doctrine and Covenants* Section 78:9.

6. Joseph Smith, *The Pearl of Great Price—A Selection from the revelations, translations, and narrations of Joseph Smith* (Salt Lake City: Church of Jesus Christ of Latter-Day Saints, 1921), 53–56.

7. See Jerald and Sandra Tanner, *3913 Changes in the Book of Mormon* (Salt Lake City: Utah Lighthouse, 1996).

8. Tanner, *3913 Changes*, 18, in the Photo Reprint section.

9. Ibid., 19.

10. Ibid., 52.

11. Ibid.

12. Ibid., 216.

13. Ibid., 218.

14. See note 5 above.

15. Urim and thummim are seer stones said to have been found with the gold plates that enabled Joseph Smith to translate the *Book of Mormon. The Pearl of Great Price—A Selection from the revelations, translations, and narrations of Joseph Smith* (Salt Lake City: Church of Jesus Christ of Latter-Day Saints, 1921), 51. Actually, the urim and thummim were stones on the breastplate of the high priest in Israel (Exodus 28:30; Leviticus 8:8). Urim means lights, and thummim means perfections according to the Hebrew and Chaldee Dictionary accompanying *Strong's Exhaustive Concordance* (McLean, VA: MacDonald Publishing, 1986) 10, 125.

16. Joseph Smith Jun., translator, *Book of Mormon* (Salt Lake City: Church of Jesus Christ of Latter-Day Saints, 1923), 478.

17. Ibid., 478.

18. Joseph Smith, *The Pearl of Great Price—A Selection from the revelations, translations, and narrations of Joseph Smith* (Salt Lake City: Church of Jesus Christ of Latter-Day Saints, 1921), 55–56.
19. Joseph Smith Jun., translator, *Book of Mormon* (Salt Lake City: Church of Jesus Christ of Latter-Day Saints, 1923) 211–12.
20. Ibid, 61.

CHAPTER 3

1. Joseph Smith (with some additions by his successors), *The Doctrine and Covenants* (Salt Lake City: Church of Jesus Christ of Latter-Day Saints, 1921), 135.
2. Ibid., 223.
3. Ibid., 166.
4. Ibid.
5. Ibid., 144–45.
6. Smith, *Book of Mormon*, 56.

CHAPTER 4

1. Merrill F. Unger, *Unger's Bible Dictionary* (Chicago: Moody Press, 1977), 889.
2. Joseph Smith (with some additions by his successors), *The Doctrine and Covenants* (Salt Lake City: Church of Jesus Christ of Latter-Day Saints, 1921), 191.
3. Ibid., 141.
4. Ibid., 33.
5. Ibid.
6. Ibid., 32.
7. Ibid., 195.
8. Ibid., 75.
9. Ibid., 196.
10. Ibid., 32, 74, 85, 61, 63, 65.
11. Ibid., 194.
12. Ibid., 192.

13. Ibid., 141.
14. Ibid., 111.
15. Ibid., 225–26.
16. Ibid., 195–97.

CHAPTER 5

1. *Greek-English Lexicon*, 240. Used with permission.
2. *Pearl of Great Price*, 48.
3. *Greek-English Lexicon*, 881.
4. *Doctrine and Covenants*, 33.
5. Ibid., 141.
6. Ibid., 32–33.

CHAPTER 6

1. R. Laird Harris, Gleason L. Archer, Jr., and Bruce K. Waltke, *Theological Wordbook of the Old Testament* (Chicago: Moody Bible Institute, 1980), 862.

CHAPTER 7

1. Other attributes of God could be mentioned such as patience and kindness, but those in the chart are chosen to be representative of the moral nature of God.

CPSIA information can be obtained
at www.ICGtesting.com
Printed in the USA
LVHW091012171219
640775LV00001B/116/P

9 781973 670261